ExVangelical

I0162889

Seven
Steps to
Leaving
Evangelical
Christianity

Without

Losing
Your
Faith

CONTEMPLATIVE
CHRISTIANS.COM

Books by Peter Traben Haas

Contemplative Church:
How Meditative Prayer and Monastic Practices Help
Congregations Flourish

The God Who Is Here:
A Contemplative Guide to Transforming Your
Relationship with God and the Church

Centering Prayers:
A One-Year Daily Companion for Going Deeper
into the Love of God

Centering Prayers VOL. 2:
Daily Peace for Turbulent Times

A Beautiful Prayer:
Answering Common Misperceptions about
Centering Prayer

A Living Lent:
A Contemplative Daily Companion
for Lent and Holy Week

My Yes Is Yours:
A Contemplative Daily Companion
for Advent and Christmas

The Advent Remedy:
A Contemplative Daily Reader
for Advent and Christmas

EXVANGELICAL

SEVEN STEPS TO LEAVING EVANGELICAL CHRISTIANITY WITHOUT LOSING YOUR FAITH

PETER TRABEN HAAS

Peter Traben Haas
Published by ContemplativeChristians.com

ExVangelical: *Seven Steps to Leaving Evangelical Christianity Without Losing Your Faith*

© 2021 Peter Traben Haas. All rights reserved. Published 2021.

No part of this publication may be reproduced, stored in a retrieval system, or transmitted in any form or by any means, except as permitted under Section 107 or 108 of the 1976 United States Copyright Act, without prior written permission of the Author or Publisher.

Unless otherwise noted, Scripture references are taken from the New Revised Standard Version. All rights reserved.

Library of Congress Cataloging-in-Publication Data

Haas, Peter Traben
ExVangelical: *Seven Steps to Leaving Evangelical Christianity Without Losing Your* Faith

ISBN: 978-0-578-75800-8

p.cm.
1.Spiritual life – Christianity. 2. Contemplative. I. Title. BV 4501.4.H35 2021
Printed in the United States of America

**Dedicated to Evangelical Mentors
& Teachers –**

Stuart Briscoe
Joe Stowell
Alistair Begg
Ravi Zacharias
Greg Quiggle
Dennis Fisher
David Kearns-Preston
David Williams
James Richards

Esteemed pastors and professors, who first inspired
me in faith and knowledge. All, men of God, who
modeled Moody Bible Institute's motto:

> *"Do your best to present yourself to God
> as one approved, a worker who does not
> need to be ashamed and who correctly
> handles the word of truth."*

– 2 Timothy 2.15

Contents

Introduction 11

Step #1 It is OK to see God differently 21

Step #2 It is OK to see the Bible differently 33

Step #3 It is OK to see salvation differently, Pt. 1 47

Step #3 It is OK to see salvation differently, Pt.2 63

Step #4 It is OK to see the earth differently 81

Step #5 It is OK to see prayer differently 99

Step#6 It is OK to see sex differently 111

Step #7 It is OK to see your destiny differently 133

"Each stage [of human development] …incorporates and builds on the structures of the previous stages, integrating them into a more comprehensive and versatile new stage."

- Lawrence Kohlberg, in James Fowler, *Stages of Faith*, 79.

Introduction

I am not against anyone or any kind of Christianity.

I am for a deepening, growing faith experience and relationship with God in the Way of Jesus Christ, by the Holy Spirit which at its heart is the goal of contemplative Christianity.

Thus, I offer these thoughts in service to anyone who is seeking a way forward deeper in their faith, not an end to it.

I'm also writing this because it feels to me that Christianity, and especially Evangelical Christianity, is reaching an evolutionary tipping point.

I would like to be a part of the conversation that helps find a way forward in faith. I'd like to help people of faith suffer less than I did in my passage through a certain kind of Christian ethos we call broadly, and (admittedly) vaguely, "Evangelical." Perhaps this resource can help ease your frustration and provide helpful counsel amidst an increasing sense of spiritual confusion.

It turned out that on my spiritual journey most of Evangelical Christianity's perspectives did not make sense to me. So, after a long time struggling, I gave up trying to get the circle of faith to fit into the square of rationality.

The more I surrendered trying to figure it all out, the more I was given help.

The help I found is called the contemplative dimension of Christianity. I believe its wisdom is useful in this season of spiritual and cultural friction and evolution.

I am not trying to start a fight with anyone. There is freedom in choosing what one believes and how one chooses to perceive human experience, including its spiritual dimension.

I aim to tell my story and share the steps along the way where I discern my own growth happened, and how my thinking, faith and growth unfolded and evolved. Perhaps my journey exemplifies some of the inherent tensions and problems within the Evangelical level of consciousness (i.e. way of seeing things).

My growth took time. It was a process, but eventually I discovered a different kind of Christianity, and as I have looked back upon my spiritual journey, I am grateful for the foundation I was given by the Evangelical perspective and community.

I am also grateful for the way out and the way forward the contemplative dimension provided me when I came to the edge of my being and knew that what I had known and believed as the Evangelical perspective was no longer workable for me.

This book is an attempt to share my story and seven of the important steps along the way of my faith formation. Here is an overview of the steps:

Step #1 It is OK to see God differently

Step #2 It is OK to see the Bible differently

Step #3 It is OK to see salvation differently

Step #4 It is OK to see the earth differently

Step #5 It is OK to see prayer differently

Step#6 It is OK to see sex differently

Step #7 It is OK to see your destiny differently

To begin, we will start with a presupposition and a claim and then conclude with an analogy and a few of my credentials.

A presupposition: Evangelical Christianity is an expression of one popular and cultural level of consciousness *among many possible levels of consciousness.* It is one way of seeing things. Evangelical Christianity is not the fourth member of the Holy Trinity. Nor is it the 67th book of the Holy Bible.

Like most everything else in the field of human culture and knowledge, whatever Evangelical Christianity is, it is most certainly a limited manifestation of multiple human perceptions congealed into what we call a worldview, or meme, or level of consciousness.

A claim: No one is really designed to remain at the Evangelical level of consciousness. We are created as self-developing organisms. Spiritual fruitfulness requires growth and evolution. Development is not static. It is dynamic and diverse.

In my interactions with Evangelical Christians, including my own personal experience within the Evangelical mindset, I have discerned tacit internal dissonance about the Evangelical way of being Christian, whether admitted or understood.

The question is how much and how long such feelings of dissonance are ignored, repressed, or contorted into defensive behavior.

Many people have a vested financial and personal interest in keeping the Evangelical movement or institution or level of consciousness fixed and strong. As a result, they often place limitations on the extent they are willing to grow beyond their current level of perception and understanding. That is OK, but we need to put our preferences and agendas on the table and recognize that for many, faith often means fossilization. And that prevents flourishing.

An analogy. Please do not take this personally or literally. It is an analogy. Evangelical Christianity is a developmental stage of faith, like 6th grade is a stage of learning on the journey to post-graduate study.

No one who wishes to grow stays in grade school. Everyone who wishes to grow graduates to higher/deeper levels of being and understanding. This is a fact. I don't assume I have reached the deepest level of learning. That doesn't happen in this lifetime.

Everyone living is still on a journey of discovery. We are all open systems capable of further growth, development and indeed transformation. (If you doubt this read James Fowler's helpful book *Stages of Faith* and notice which stage you become uncomfortable with or disagree with as you read. The stage prior to where you became uncomfortable is probably a good guide to where you are at developmentally and an invitation to keep growing).

Here are a few of my credentials. I grew up a child of the Jesus' People movement, with parents who were participants of several prominent evangelical Christian communities and bands (such as Rez Band and Servant). I grew up at Elmbrook Church under the tutelage of Stuart and Jill Briscoe's profound biblical preaching. I graduated with a dual bachelor's degree in Bible and Theology from the West Point Academy of Evangelical, Biblical Christianity: Moody Bible Institute.

Not only that, during my senior year at Moody I was the student body president. In my junior year I founded the Student Academic Club. I also started a ministry to the homeless my freshman year. I am a MDiv graduate of Princeton Seminary. I've earned a Doctor of Ministry. I have been an ordained Presbyterian pastor for nearly 30 years. I currently serve a contemplative friendly church in Colorado. Perhaps I should also add, "and I have from time to time been "a Pharisee of Pharisees."

While at Moody, trying to be a good bible evangelical, I had a crisis of faith and intellect. It was a slow process, like all healthy growth is. The process of my transformation, and dare I say liberation, began during my Church History 101 class with the illuminating lectures of Dr. Greg Quiggle. It deepened in Philosophy 101 class with the brilliant Dr. Doug Kennard. And it came to full fruition the summer after graduating when I became an atheist for a day. But more on that later.

For two of the four years of my time at Moody in Chicago I worshipped at a conservative Presbyterian Church (PCA). But I couldn't comprehend why there weren't any women in leadership. So, one night, I took a courageous step and visited a magnificent church (I was nervous since folks at Moody referred to it as a liberal church).

I went to the Sunday evening vespers service at the Fourth Presbyterian Church on Michigan Avenue across the street from the John Hancock Building.

As worship began, I was moved to tears by the beauty of the candle lit sanctuary. My heart was flooded with joy and awe as a woman pastor stood up in her black Geneva gown and white Geneva tabs and with outstretched arms said, "Welcome to the House of God to Worship our God of Love." We served the homeless dinner after worship; that sealed it for me. I joined Fourth Presbyterian Church a month later.

After Moody, I took a year off prior to going to seminary to work at an excellent Evangelical mega church in Brookfield, Wisconsin called Elmbrook. I worked there as a pastoral resident. The residency was designed to help me discern if I was called to the pastorate by getting broad pastoral experience. I also was using it as a test to explore if I could go the Evangelical route versus the denominational, Presbyterian route.

It was 1995. During that year, watching the increasingly personality driven showmanship of mega churches nationwide, and seeing the worship trends changing more toward the theatre and production experience, I decided that there was no way I could continue down the Evangelical route. That way of doing and being church was not for me.

Sure enough, nearly 40 years since then much of Evangelical, nondenominational style of worship has been concertized and moodifed with dark rooms, stage lighting and expensive multi-media systems and imagery – essentially becoming multi-media production events. As different as the cell phone is to the telegraph. Today, in the wake of Covid-19 has virtually turned every church or congregation into a live-streamed, virtual community. It is game changing stuff – and most churches can't keep up.

The consumerism draped in spirituality turned me off at Moody. It still does. In fact, sadly, I think it is worse today than ever. I call it the "Walmartization" of Christianity. Big box churches with even bigger parking lots with even bigger egos on the stage or screens, or so it seems to me.

That is not to say the denominational world is any better. The last 50 years or so have seen precipitous declines in denominational congregations.

My own life and ministry is lacking too and were it not for my own breakdown I'm sure I'd still be inflated with my false self too trying to perform with "big screens" and keep up appearances. More too on that later.

All this to say, I have been so blessed to discover the contemplative dimension hiding in plain sight all along, moving beyond both denominationalism and evangelicalism.

The contemplative dimension has helped me stay rooted in my own tradition and not leave the pastorate altogether. It also was the bridge I needed to leave the unworkable perspectives of my Evangelical Christian land of birth and lead me deeper into the promised land that was waiting for my inward attention all along.

These essays were originally written in 2012 as a part of a blog series with ContemplativeChristians.com. They are available here in published form, with some hesitation, but this season of life seems particularly in need of such a resource, and is offered in the spirit of self-disclosure in service to the unfolding journeys of others seeking a deeper way amidst the confusion.

Peter Traben Haas

Step #1:
It is OK to see God differently

How a person understands God, tells a lot about how they might understand themselves. The two are often interconnected. Our views of God and our theological understanding and our knowledge of self tend to grow, shift and change throughout our life, in tandem.

Since how we understand and see God is such a foundational step in the process of evolving human faith and development, we begin here.

On my spiritual journey, I began to see God differently in five areas. And it was my fascination with the night sky that first prompted deeper questions.

While we all tend to inherit our initial God-view from our family of origin, early religious education, experiences/practices, worship, or the culture and religion we are raised in, one of the dominant worldviews we have inherited in the last one-hundred years or so, is the increasing awareness that not only is the earth *not* the center of the solar system, the solar system is not the center of the galaxy.

Indeed, most people are *just now* beginning to understand that we are part of a vast, expanding universe, and it is to this new cosmological dimension that we turn to now on our evolving journey through and beyond Evangelical Christianity.

Cosmos

My first perception of God was that God lived up in the church nave, where high above the Lord's Table at the pinnacle of the ceiling there was a door, or what looked like a door to my five-year-old mind. I remember loving being in the sanctuary of Elm Grove Lutheran Church and looking up at the door thinking "that is where God lives and through that door I can get to heaven."

When I was seven years old, my mother told me one summer night as we were camping on the shores of Lake Michigan that the shining stars were holes in the floor of heaven, letting heaven's light through. I believed her, but I also wondered what is beyond heaven? These are impressions of an enduring perspective within the monotheistic traditions that God is "up there."

The "up-there" perspective of God is discerned in many places in Western culture – most famously in Michelangelo's rendering of God reaching down to humankind painted on the ceiling of the Sistine Chapel. It is also recognizable in less lofty expressions such as "talk to the big guy up-stairs."

There are many scriptures that have innocently fostered this "up-there" perspective, such as Jacob's Ladder and Jesus' Ascension.

Nevertheless, much of the biblical cosmology conveys a pre-modern view that is no longer workable in the post-Hubble Telescope era.

The earth-centered view with a God "above" us in "heaven" reached through various "doorways" in the sky or "stairways" up to the next realm can't fully convey the tremendous mystery of a visible universe nearly 14 billion light years in scale, expanding in every direction at the speed of light.

So, as I began to read books like Cletus Wessels', *The Holy Web: Church and the New Universe Story*, the writings of Pierre Teilhard de Chardin and Ilia Delio, I began to see God's presence differently. I began to see God less like an old man with a white beard sitting on a throne "up-there," and more like the Source of life, light, and love.

This transition in my perspective of God also made sense in what I was learning about human development from psychologist James Fowler in his book *Stages of Faith*.

That book, and the writings of Clare Graves and Ken Wilber, helped me see that my shift was not so much heretical or even "losing my faith," but more so the wonderful and inevitable upsurge of human development calling me to grow.

The charge against this new view and understanding of God as Source is often that it is simply panentheism reframed. Meaning that everything is in God.

That is almost what I am saying, but not quite. We need to add the Trinity as the lens of perception. What I believe and sometimes experience as the fruit of contemplative prayer is that everything can now be in Christ and that Christ, the union of the human and divine, revealed and modeled in Jesus, is emerging into all and everything in the wake of the resurrection and ascension events.

Or as St. Paul put it, "that Christ might be all in all" (1 Corinthians 15.28). Accepting this view also required a deeper shift in my understanding of the Trinity. Which leads me to my second perception of God.

Trinity

My second perception of God was related to the first. Coupled with my reading of the Trinitarian thinking of T.F. Torrance, Colin Gunton, James Loder, and especially the helpful book by James Torrance, *Worship, Community and the Triune God of Grace*, over a period of several years a very compelling and life-giving Trinitarian, relational perspective of God began to emerge from the earlier formation of God as an old man with a beard sitting on a throne in heaven, with a Jewish man about thirty sitting beside him, and a white dove hovering nearby.

The Trinitarian insights helped me out of the static perspective of the "up-there God" that looks like this:

God
|
Jesus
|
Me

I particularly found James Torrance's critique of the Evangelical "Jesus worship" extremely helpful in describing my own deepening hunger for a fuller perspective of the Trinity in worship and in prayer. I wanted more of God, not less. I wanted more than just Jesus devotion.

The insights of the Eastern church fathers such as Gregory of Nyssa and Gregory of Nazianzus were helpful in giving me a theological vision of God that was a feast for my soul. If I had more courage back then, I probably would have converted to Eastern Orthodoxy or at least Roman Catholicism.

If there is a non-literal analogy that conveys to me the insights of the shift in cosmology connected with a deepening understanding of the Trinity, it is the analogy of a Russian Nesting doll – one hidden within the other. Unity in diversity. It is a simple and limiting analogy, but it helps.

The analogy breaks down because the levels or "energies" or "persons" of God aren't really separated, they are interrelated. The technical word for this is Perichoresis. A better analogy might be a cell within an organ within a body. But that analogy also breaks down since the cell is not equal to the body, whereas each "Energy" of the Trinity is co-equal.

But at least these analogies begin to introduce co-indwelling and interrelatedness, breaking the stranglehold of just a "Jesus and me" mentality. The Trinitarian model helped me move deeper into the richness of the Christian revelation Jesus came to demonstrate and for humankind to experience and replicate.

When we look at the universe now, we also see this interrelatedness: systems within systems, with parts that form the totality of the whole. And perhaps there are universes within universes!

The ancient esoteric insight conveyed by Jesus in his teaching on prayer, "as above, so below" (Matthew 6.10), teaches us that there is much we can learn from the "book of the universe" about our perspectives of God.

Nothing

The third shift in perspective of God came as I began to read the writings of John of the Cross, Teresa of Avila, and the modern contemplative Thomas Keating.

Through these friends in faith, I was given words that helped explain my own interior experiences and longings.

If you are hungering for more of God's light, life and love, and a more vibrant spiritual faith, run, and I mean run to these writers. You might even consider watching Thomas Keating's profound yet dated video series called *The Spiritual Journey*. If I had seen this when I was twenty years old, perhaps I would have been saved a great deal of inner anguish on my journey.

My exposure to these and other contemplative writers and practices may have been the most important shift of all. And I will try to explain it, but it is difficult to do so with words. And if I offend anyone, I ask your forgiveness.

My aim is to share my story so that it might help others avoid the difficulties and heartache I experienced feeling so lost and uncertain where I belonged in the multi-faceted Christian cosmos.

The contemplative (apophatic) dimension of Christianity helped me remember and experience the freeing truth that God does not need anything. In the depths of silence and solitude, I remember that perhaps:

God does not need to be defended or for nations to be claimed for Christ.

God does not even need me to tell another person about Jesus.

God does not need the Bible.

God does not need the church.

God does not need money, armies, guns or holy wars.

God does not need me to be cool, hip or trendy and become a "successful" evangelist or pastor.

God does not need to win elections or legislative victories.

God is fine without us and our big ministry plans, missional endeavors and religiously motivated political agendas.

So, I have come to understand that we can relax. Or, as the scriptures put it, "be still and know that I am God" (Psalm 42.1).

In my view, the problem is that we tend to make God in our image. Perhaps we made God into a consumer who needs things. The contemplative dimension helped me see that:

God is infinite supply, not infinite need.

Infinite grace, not infinite demand.

Infinite love, not unrelenting fear or judgement.

As I began to see God differently from the perspective of contemplative experiences, it inevitably began to shift how I saw myself and others. I'll share more on that later. In short, it began to turn me more into love. I began to see that I needed to purge.

I purged a lot of fear-based presuppositions about God and myself accumulated over my first thirty years of life. Remembering that God is God and doesn't need anything was a helpful initial reset, especially since so much of the American evangelical empire I experienced seemed to be built upon the subtle notion that God needed us to do stuff and be successful at it.

In fact, in my experience the shadow message within the Evangelical Christianity was that God needed us to win. I noticed all the strategies for succeeding, summiting, leading, influencing, impacting, and living my best life now. For example, I have never met a mega church that didn't message the gospel in this "success" way. They might cloak it in spiritual terms such as multiplication, reaping the harvest, sowing the seed, or a season of God's favor. In contrast, I have never met a monastery that did.

Why this fascination with largeness? With numbers? With success? Why the fascination with bigness? With membership? With numerical growth? During my years at Moody and in my interactions with multiple American mega-churches, I experienced a tacit view of God that says: Bigger is better. More is better. Win as many souls as you can!

Success is numerical growth. Keep worship looking new, young, and exciting. Keep building. Keep striving. I have no idea about people's motivations. I am just noticing trends in my experiences. I am also *not* saying that we should just become passive quietists or slip away into irrelevancy.

I am saying perhaps we need a shift of perspective about what our role is as participants in the divine nature (2 Peter 1.4). Participants don't do it all. They participate in what has already been done and undone for them.

Night

Let's look at the key perspective of brokenness. During my frustrations with that kind of "success" mentality, I had a breakdown. I recommend having a breakdown. That's right: I think it is developmentally useful to realize that your system of faith isn't God and can be very healthy to let it (or parts of it) go. This kind of spiritual evolution will often require, to varying degrees, a crisis of faith.

For me, during my 20's I had multiple little breakdowns. Little seasons of angst that helped undo my false self and its subtle attachments to a Christianity that tried to avoid such weakness or ineffectiveness, cloaked in wealth, fame, or power.

Such moments or seasons of break downs are what the tradition calls, "dark nights of the soul," or more simply – purgation. I wish I had known that at the time. I thought what I was experiencing was unique. Turns out, it happens all the time. It is a vital part of the spiritual journey and developmental process.

A spiritual crisis in service to our transformation and development happens when we begin to accept that our view of our self is too big, and our view of God isn't big enough. It begins to happen when we let go of the homemade self and truly live by faith in the midst of the darkness of un-knowing and purgation.

The "night" won't last forever. It will pass. The contemplative dimension of the Christian tradition reminded me that in order to be birthed into more maturity in Christ, my perspective and understanding of God required little deaths and resurrections, both spiritually and psychologically. Instead of repressing it or running away from the false self and all its perspectives, I began to feel the fear and the strivings of the falseness. It was the beginning of a new life.

Most likely you will not have to go looking for a breakdown or crisis. It will come to you in the normal process of human development from adolescence to adulthood.

It often happens in college when our childhood faith is tested by adulthood knowledge. Or at midlife when our pursuit of happiness on our own terms becomes unworkable and our life hits a wall of opposition or a cliff of despair. Whenever it occurs, it is an important opportunity not to throw one's faith out, but rather to work out our faith through the frictions.

As best as I can tell, growth requires receiving new information and transcending the old not by getting rid of the old, but by incorporating the new. This is a creative, life-giving process, although it may feel like hell at the time.

Abba

Finally, I never could have made it through my seasons of purgation and transition without the wisdom of a spiritual father or mother. If you don't have one, I highly suggest asking God in prayer to give you a wise spiritual father or mother. A spiritual mentor or guide. No matter how old you are, we need wise spiritual fathers and mothers who are at a higher/deeper level of understanding and spiritual Being than we are at. Request a spiritual father or mother. Spend time with them and accept the fact that they are at a higher/deeper/fuller understanding and being than you. Learn from them.

Meeting and being with a more developed, mature, holy, wise spiritual father or mother can keep us humble and help us journey through the different perspectives of God and the customary purgations along our spiritual journey and development.

Step #2
It is OK to see the Bible differently

First, let's start out with a personal example that I hope sets the tone of reverence that I have for the scriptures. Since I was seventeen years old, I have been writing daily devotionals for myself in a journal. I read a passage of scripture(s) and listen to it and then write about what I am hearing and receiving from the text. There are twenty volumes of notebooks in my closet.

I am not bragging, but I am trying to alert the reader that I am not a Bible basher. If I missed a few days of Bible study, I felt like I was running on thin air, gasping for oxygen. I love the Bible. It is just I've come to love God more.

However, in recent years, I have increasingly stopped reading and writing so much and have shifted to the practice of lectio divina, a longstanding Christian practice that nurtures simply resting with God's Word instead of trying to master it.

I seek to live and move and have my being in the energetic field of the risen Christ, experienced in a five-fold spectrum composed of a perichoretic harmony of the following expressions, which, to my surprise, also happens to follow what the monastic tradition has been doing all along:

Listening to and meditating upon Scripture with the ear of the heart.

Drawing deeply from the Christian Wisdom tradition (i.e. Maurice Nicoll).

Resting in the heart of God's love through a twice daily contemplative prayer practice (Centering Prayer and Jesus' Prayer).

Participating in Eucharistic liturgy.

Consenting to become love and sharing loving service to others.

This fivefold path wasn't always the case for me.

For the first eighteen years of my life, I thought the Bible dropped out of heaven. Literally. Then I learned that the Bible didn't exist in its present "compiled" form until the 3rd or 4th century C.E., at least 250 years after the death of Jesus.

In fact, Jesus didn't have the Bible we have. Nor did the any of the apostles. What they mostly had access to were various scrolls or sections of the Torah, the Hebrew scriptures.

Foundations are everything, and when what you thought was your foundation (i.e. the inerrant Bible) starts to crumble in college, can we understand why so many begin to also lose their faith? It was a big set-up. And it didn't have to be this way.

My critique of the Fundamentalists meetings around 1900 was that the power of fear led them to make a little paper god out of the Bible. Rather than thinking more deeply about the issues of the day, such as evolution, psychological insights, and the growing knowledge of ancient cultures and archeology, they chose to ensconce themselves in doctrines, build their own schools and separate out from the culture as if in exile.

In college I began to learn about the "attacks" on the Bible from textual critics to liberal philosophers. I began to learn about the increasing historical, archeological and textual critiques of the Bible. It started to disrupt my faith, and I didn't know how to process the fact that the Bible wasn't the perfect inerrant document I had been taught to believe it was. What is an eighteen-year-old to do when the thing he has put his faith in on par with God is shown to be less than perfect, and many times very uninspired and uninspiring?

What I did was spend the summer after my freshman year reading and studying about the Bible. I read books like *Evidence that Demands a Verdict* by Josh McDowell and *The New Testament Documents: Are They Reliable* by F.F. Bruce. I read books by leading biblical scholars like Bruce Metzger and Tom Wright. I still have the 100-page research paper I wrote that summer on the subject trying to answer my own questions about the bible. My study gave me sufficient reason to trust the scriptures, at least from a textual perspective.

By this time, I understood that the documents comprising the Bible were written by human beings over a long period of time and collated by others over a similar period of time, and that the documents reflected the concerns and perspectives of the time(s) in which the texts were written.

That is not to say some of the scriptures don't speak to us today as if inspired by higher influences. They do. It is just that I slowly began to see that my faith was never meant to be in a book or even in written words. The book informs me about what I believe and experience, but I don't really have a relationship with texts or even words.

I have a relationship with God through the living Christ by word, silence and sacrament in the grace of the Holy Spirit.

The written words of the Bible became for me symbols conveying grace and meaning. I discovered that the meanings often changed depending on my internal state of receptivity and how attentively I was listening to the Spirit through the written word of God.

I've also begun to understand how important it is for us to teach the Bible to children in developmentally appropriate ways.

A Protestant Pope

During my freshman year at Moody I worked a part-time job that involved going up to the executive suites occasionally – the board room, the office of the president, legal counsel, etc. One day, I walked by the boardroom, and the door was open.

And without trying to, there in plain view for any passerby to see was an easel with the following words in large letters on it, clearly left from an envisioning meeting: "The Five Distinctions of Moody" The first distinction on the paper was this: The authority of Scripture is primary.

At the time, I remember thinking, "wow, they really have their act together." Over the years, I have remembered that experience and respected their clarity of mission. In fact, I'm so grateful to Moody for that clarity, and many other reasons.

Soon I began to experience interior dissonance with the authority of scripture though.

The more I learned about the Bible, the more the dissonance increased. Indeed, the more I really read the Bible, so too the dissonance grew in volume.

In fact, this one concept, "the authority of scripture at all costs" was the taproot for so much of my interior anguish as a younger man, trying to fit the world of the Bible into the world of the 1990's.

By the time I graduated from Moody, I was able to see that the real problem with the fundamentalist authority of Scripture viewpoint isn't the Bible itself, it is that the Bible never claims for itself the kind of authority most of American Protestantism has given it.

Many have written about this, and I won't go into the historical and intellectual stream that led to the fundamentalist exaltation of the Bible as a Protestant Pope.

What I will say is that everything in nature has a center. Look at an image of the Milky Way galaxy, or a human cell, or a hurricane, a flower, an embryo. Everything has a center. And if it doesn't, it falls apart. So too in human social and belief systems.

When the Protestant and Reformed movements disconnected from the gravity of the center of authority that was and is the Pope, the Bishop of Rome, or Patriarch of Constantinople, etc. there was a significant vacuum of authority created. It was filled, for a time by charismatic leaders such as Luther and Calvin. But leaders come and go. So, what would become the center holding the Protestant movement together?

Some might say, Jesus! Perhaps, but in my reading and experience it seems to me that the new center for the Protestant church, became the bible, the Protestant Pope.

The printing press made this more possible, enabling everyone who wanted to read the Bible to do so. Thus, in time, the primary hallmark of the Protestant style, and especially the American Fundamentalist style of Christianity, including its younger sister, Evangelicalism, was the authority of the Bible.

A twin to the authority of the Bible was the lens by which the Fundamentalist movement chose to interpret the Bible with. The primary lens of scripture interpretation during my years at Moody and at many self-defined Evangelical churches I experienced, both small and massive, was that "we interpret the Bible literally."

The literal lens of biblical interpretation also created immense dissonance in me because I began to see deep inconsistencies within this approach to Scripture reading. I tried to read the Bible literally, but my soul kept wanting more, insisting there was something deeper.

What was worse, it seemed to me that the literal approach didn't seem to even want to be questioned. For example, many of my questions in Bible class were often not answered in any significant way. Why might that be? Here is what I have come to believe.

Level

Let's begin with an analogy. If you live in an area where the highway goes through a hilly spot, and they had to cut away the earth for the road, perhaps you have seen the earth's layers exposed.

There is section of road that I frequently drive by. It looks like a layered cake, with different colors of rock every three or four feet. It is called rock strata, and it is like information burned on a CD track – each track containing different information about the history of the earth and that geological time period. These layers of rock are levels of time and space, deposited for us to now see and study.

In a similar way the geologic record reveals much about the past state of the earth, so too does the textual record reveal much about the state of human culture, thought and understanding. Books are like rock cut-outs. They reveal what was happening in the past. They reveal how people were thinking about themselves and about God.

Another way of saying this is that the Bible is a written record of human development, especially human levels of perception or consciousness.

I often ask people when I talk about this, "why Didn't God just start out with Jesus?" It would have saved a lot of time and effort, and if you read the book of Joshua, it would have saved a lot of blood and innocent animal life! Why start with Noah or Abraham? Why start with animal sacrifice?

Why not just start with the Jesus? Why did God wait for so many centuries so that, "in the fullness of time" God would send the Son? Here is one way I answer that important question: because humankind wasn't ready.

Here is another non-literal, non-personal analogy. We don't teach our 1st graders trigonometry, but we do teach our high school juniors trigonometry. Why? Because we only teach learner ready information.

In a similar way, God was accommodating to the developmental level of humankind, laying down the tracks so that one day the engine of Christ might run on them.

It took time. God accommodated to human consciousness, and in the fullness of time, that is to say, when human consciousness was ready to receive the Christ, it happened. That is one reason why the Hebrew Scriptures (the Old Testament) is so different from the Christian scriptures. It's a developmental record of consciousness.

One is not worse than the other. They complement each other, just as our earlier years complement our later years. In fact, we probably wouldn't be where we are now without that which preceded our present state. It is an earlier part comprising the continuously expanding whole.

So, it is not appropriate to treat the whole Bible the same. While all of scripture might be God-breathed, just like all the universe is, no one thinks the earth is the same as the moon. We treat different dimensions differently. Which gets us to the matter of interpretation.

Lenses

Not only are there levels of consciousness embedded in the depository record of texts, but there are also levels of interpretation within the human reading of those texts.

In practice, I've not known any evangelical pastor who has *only* interpreted the Bible literally from the pulpit. All the preaching I have ever heard has included the classical four-fold senses of interpretation: literal, allegorical, moral and anagogic.

But so much of the Evangelical culture I experienced in theory was literal. In practice, though, no one is literal 100%. They pick and choose, depending on their intention and purpose.

This is what I have come to know and believe by my own experience as a Christian and a pastor: the literal level cannot explain much of the Bible because so much of the Bible was written at a deeper, non-literal level.

The problem with so much of the Evangelical and Fundamentalist culture I experienced was not their reverence of scripture, but rather the apparent un-willingness to let the Bible be a living, symbolic text through which the Spirit speaks.

They demand that the bible be a static textbook that can hit you over the head word-for-word as if nothing has changed or not developed in five thousand years of human evolution. Furthermore, one lens will never be able to explain all the levels.

Getting to this place of understanding was not easy for me. It probably took 10 years for me to be free from the fear that I was not reading scripture correctly and that I was a heretic white washer whose soul was in jeopardy because I was shifting in my understanding of our use of the Bible.

This is a key distinction. The problem is not with the Bible. The problems occur with our use of the Bible. And what is the source of our use of the Bible if not the interior state of human consciousness formed by intellectual layers of education and the maturity of one's Understanding which is the sum total of one's knowledge and being. In our normal waking state, we are always in between the text and the interpretation.

The one who reads (subject) can never be separated from that which is read (object). There is a deep interplay between the two. There is always a someone in between the text and the interpretation and that someone (or self) has a level of consciousness influencing everything that someone sees, thinks, and feels.

The profound insight provided to me by the wisdom of the contemplative tradition was to cease trying to master the text through my scholarly interpretation and let the text master me.

Instead of me reading the text the text is reading me. This shifted the entire game for me, inviting me into a deeper integration of myself and a much more joyful demeanor in relationship with the world. This is a subtle yet profound shift, and difficult to describe with words, but it is available for anyone to experience.

God's light, life and love are flowing through the text, like sunlight streaming through a window. There are times when we can't tell the difference between the light and the windowpane. They seem totally one, like a hypostatic union. Spirit and Text, Wisdom and Written Word.

This is moving toward the mystical dimension, where more than we ask or imagine is possible, including revelation and divine encounter with the living Jesus Christ. But that is beyond what I may speak of.

The contemplative dimension helped me hear that the drumbeat of God's message is also beating beyond the pages of scripture. The Spirit is still speaking to us, just as music still lingers in the heart long after the symphony ends.

It is the echo of God's voice as deep calls to deep. It is unmistakable. God is still speaking in words recorded long ago, and in words whispered in the still place of the soul right now, especially the broken-hearted soul.

Will the church and its leaders have the courage to let go of our fears and need to control and trust the one whose living words ignite a burning of the heart and soul (Luke 24.13 – 35)?

Or will we keep trying to kill the mystics and prophets? "O Jerusalem, Jerusalem! You fear the very thing you need!"

Illumination and inspiration are never limited to scripture or past revelation, but available relationally with Christ by the Spirit here and now. Ask. Seek. Knock.

This is the miracle of God's light, life, and love among us by the Spirit, and no religious authority or theological system can cease the Spirit's free flow to and through us bringing wisdom and truth. It is lawful.

Truth permeates the cosmos and is available in the knowledge incarnated in both the living and written word of God.

Step #3
It is OK to see salvation differently, **Part 1**

A Disclaimer

For me, Jesus the Christ is the demonstration of the fullness of human life, and an evolutionary tipping point that is slowly transforming humankind forward into a further dimension of consciousness (i.e., way of seeing) and understanding of God, ourselves, our universe and destiny.

For my understanding, the resurrection of Jesus the Christ is the Center and central hope of and for the human experience on planet earth – psychologically, spiritually, physically, and culturally.

What follows is not a rejection of the Christian story. It is an interpretation of it. This is about what style of Christianity I have been drawn toward and seek to embody.

By default, it is also a story about the style of Christianity I have moved away from. I claim no authority other than that I experience myself as a child of God and hold within my heart the name of Jesus Christ. I am a simple follower of Jesus, the foot washer. My aim is not to be right, but to become love.

My wish is to help others on their journey, lessening their time and suffering in the normal process and confusions of development from one level of being to another. I understand that I am not the only one seeking for a deeper, more life-giving expression of Christianity. Yes, these are confusing times. But they are also ripe with possibilities for personal and communal transformation.

I do not view this as a neo-gnostic project for an elite few of enlightened beings. Rather, I believe growth is a possibility for all humankind, symbolized by Jesus' invitation to "abide" and "bear fruit" (John 15), as well as the Divine invitation at the beginning of the biblical story to "be fruitful and grow!" (Genesis 1.28).

I'm curious if humankind and especially "evangelical" Christians will open to deeper understandings emerging in our era through the grace of God helping us to mature into the full stature of Christ, moving beyond our earlier, evangelical and emergent growth?

Can we do this without reacting in fear and labeling people like me as arrogant and misguided heretics? Perhaps that will be a possibility. But I also remember this phrase: "O Jerusalem, O Jerusalem, (i.e., O religious establishment), why do you insist on killing the prophets" who are simply calling to you to remember and move beyond old, unworkable ways of thinking for your own good?

Perhaps we have confused our thoughts with God.

Perhaps we have confused our systems of faith with the journey of salvation.

Perhaps we have forgotten the meaning of words meanwhile building our Christian commercial empires of power and wealth.

You will know a tree by its fruit. These reflections are, in part, my fruit. Perhaps it will seem rotten to you. Perhaps immature.

Or perhaps it will be sweet to your heart, mind and spirit. Please discern if what follows are words of light, life and love, or words of darkness, death and fear.

Don't just believe me. Verify everything in the silence of your own personal surrender to the living Presence of the Risen Jesus Christ by word, prayer and sacrament.

The Problem of Salvation

Any worthwhile doctrine of salvation accounts for two things: (1) A problem and (2) a solution.

Here are a few quotes about salvation – the problem and solution – I heard as a young man growing up in self defined Evangelical communities: "Sin separates you from God. If you confess your sin, and believe in the Lord Jesus Christ, God is faithful and will forgive you and will give you the gift of eternal life in heaven."

Or this variation:

"Believe on the Lord Jesus Christ. Come to his cross upon which he shed blood for the forgiveness of your sins. Turn from your unbelief and trust in Jesus Christ as your lord and Savior and escape the sure judgment of God and the eternal fires of Hell."

Or this:

"For God so loved the world that he gave his only Son, blameless and free from sin, to be an atonement for your sins. Trust in God's love and turn from your sins. Believe and receive Jesus. And be saved."

To varying degrees, these three quotes capture the essence of the gospel message of salvation that I heard preached in self-defined Evangelical churches during my youth and college years.   Does this language sound familiar to you?

In these constructions, the problem is sin. The solution is primarily Jesus' death on the cross, and our belief in that information, which also initiates a relationship with Jesus.

But there was a deeper problem. As I journeyed in my education and human development from adolescence to early adulthood, I increasingly became very dissatisfied with the languaging of the diagnosis and prognosis. I began to go deeper. I began to ask, "what is sin? "And "how does Jesus' death solve the sin problem?"

My questions came to the forefront when I was required to do street evangelism at Moody Bible Institute my freshman year. I found it virtually impossible to say these formulas or even use the classic five steps to peace with God tract provided for distribution to the passerby.

In fact, I thought it was a horrible thing to do to someone. Perhaps my listeners could tell because, to my great shame and guilt at the time, none of my listeners seemed to care or even comprehend what I was saying. At first, I took it personally.

I simply concluded I clearly didn't have the gift of evangelism. Or that I wasn't smart enough or quick enough on my feet.

Then, I began to see that a more truthful explanation as to why people weren't responding to my questions wasn't because of me, but because the categories of communication I was using were virtually irrelevant to the hearers.

While we all spoke English, it was if I was speaking a different language of meaning. I am not the first person to talk about this matter.

In the early 1990's Lesslie Newbigin was also writing about this. Later, it would be picked up by the Gospel and our Culture Network, which dovetailed nicely into the missional work of people like Darrell Guder and the spiritual formation work of Dallas Willard.

But back to my street evangelism. These evangelical talking points of salvation weren't intellectually or emotionally satisfying to me either. In fact, it felt more like selling something I couldn't explain, especially when a bright stranger responded to me with a question like:

 "Why do you believe God needs a blood offering?"

"How is it possible that one person's death long ago has anything to do with my life now?"

"Why are you bothering me with this. I don't need heaven right now, what I need is to be healed of cancer."

By my senior year at Moody, I had defined my difficulties with the views and "culture of salvation" I was saturated with there. Here is my short list distilled to nine. It took several years before I didn't feel like a total heretic for even asking these questions and feeling incredibly dissatisfied with the standard protestant Christian answers to them:

First, the Evangelical salvation message presupposes an acceptance or awareness of the Levitical sacrificial system: that a blood offering is required to "pay, cover, atone, or forgive" personal sins.

What are we to make of the Christian story when we no longer accept the presuppositions of a sacrificial system and see it as one phase of anthropological religious development rooted in a magical/mythical world view that no longer works in a post-modern culture?

Second, the Evangelical salvation message assumes an understanding of what sin is. When asked, sin is often defined as "separation from God." When pressed how or where this separation first occurred the answer is Adam and Eve's disobedience to God in the Garden of Eden. This was the "original sin," referred to by theologians as "The Fall."

How does that first sin continue to get passed on to every human being born since "The Fall" making us culpable and guilty? Where is this delineated or explained by the Bible? It is one thing to claim that it does get passed down. It is quite another to develop a credible theory of how in an era of sequencing of the human genome, and insights from the human social sciences.

Third, the punishment doesn't seem to fit the crime. How do we go from a story about eating the forbidden fruit to a story about needing a blood sacrifice? Clearly, there is something more going on than what the scriptures are revealing. What might that be? Is God really such a petty tyrant to demand a human death because God's offspring ate a forbidden fruit. This seems totally absurd, and if not absurd, tyrannical. With a God like that who needs an enemy!

Fourth, why is the Protestant salvation message so focused on the benefits of Jesus' death alone? Why do we focus so much on the paschal "Passover" story as the primary interpretive lens of Christianity, and not for example, on Jesus' birth or transfiguration or resurrection or ascension stories? Perhaps a rebalancing and reintegration of the full narrative is needed.

Fifth, the salvation message seems so human-centric. What about nature and planet earth? How does Jesus' death on the cross help our planet or all other living species?

Sixth, what is really happening in the Incarnation? Is Jesus here just to die for our sins? Or is there a fuller spectrum reason for the union of the human and divine natures in the one being Jesus the Christ?

Seventh, why is the focus of our salvation preaching so much about escaping a future judgment in hell and gaining the paradise of heaven? What does "salvation" have to do with my life here on planet earth right now?

Eighth, in an interconnected world of (now) seven billion people, where approximately 155,000 people die each day worldwide, many who have never heard the information that Jesus' died for their sins or believed that particular information, how do we reconcile the presupposition that unless people do hear and believe that information they do not get eternal life?

Ninth, what is the deepest aim and purpose of God's story for human destiny? Is it an evacuation plan from earth to heaven or something more?

I'll review how I have come to answer most of these questions in the next chapter, but you should know that since the early 1990's when I was a student at Moody, much has occurred to address these and similar questions.

Such as: (1) The Emergent church movement gained perhaps the most attention in the Christian "Evangelical" universe by such leader/authors as Brian McLaren and Rob Bell.

(2) So did the post-liberal movement represented by former Bishop Shelby Spong, a virtual gutting of everything Christianity holds dear. While I found Spong's complaints very compelling. articulating many of my own frustrations, the solutions left me feeling disconnected.

(3) A more recent movement was the rise of the neo-Calvinists, represented by pastor-authors Mark Driscoll and Timothy Keller.

(4) A final movement that also asks and addresses similar questions as the ones above, was the rise of the new atheism, represented by well-known authors Sam Harris and Richard Dawkins. Ana-theism has also recently emerged as an alternative story in the work of Richard Kearney.

Perhaps you have read or heard of all of these influential thought leaders. Perhaps they have also helped you, as they have me, each in their own way offering clarifying insights. A good overview of the whole emergent conversation is the book Emergence Christianity by Phyllis Tickle.

The Grammar of Salvation: John 3.16

This Gospel name and these numbers are perhaps the most well-recognized Bible reference in the world. Here is how the NIV translates this famous verse:

"For God so loved the world that he gave his one and only Son, that whoever believes in him shall not perish but have eternal life."

As I have studied this passage in the original language, I was drawn particularly to the word translated as "perish." In the Greek it is a 2nd Aorist, in the subjunctive mood. The upshot of that is that this word also conveys the meaning of losing something or of being lost, such as when we get lost in the woods.

Furthermore, not evident in the English word "perish," is the subjunctive mood the Greek is conveying.

The sense of the subjunctive mood regards the purpose or possibility of a future action. So, in my view, a better translation of the Greek word would not be "shall not perish," but rather: "may not lose oneself." That is, *may* not have a meaningless, purposeless life. The subjunctive mood is normally translated with "if" or "may" clauses. It is the mood of potential action, contingent upon certain conditions. The theological uptake is that the sense of this passage is not a certainty but a possibility.

It is possible to miss the ultimate purpose of your life which is giving yourself back to God and receiving from God the gift of the fullness of life, i.e., eternal life.

The verb could have easily been in the future tense, which does convey certainty, and is the way it is so often portrayed in the preaching I have heard. To be fair, it has also been conveyed very conditionally:

If you do this (believe)...
Then this will happen.

However, since it is in the subjunctive mood, stress should be less of a guaranteed future, and more of a purpose and possibility to take seriously.

The nuance I'm trying to attend to is that there is a purpose for trusting God with our life that can lead to significant possibilities – a life that does not reach its fullness or a life that does, and perhaps even beyond this life's fullness (John 10.10) leading to a superabundant life that both includes and transcends just this realm of existence.

The main verb of action is the Greek word *pisteuo*, translated in the NIV as "believes." Yet, what does "believe" mean? The Greek word *pisteuo* conveys the nuance of trusting.

So, I take believing to mean the willingness and consent to give oneself away. To what, though? In this case, the designation in the NIV is "in him" whoever "believes in him." Yet this prepositional pro-noun may also be translated as "to him." So, in that case we get this very startling distinction of meaning:

"God so loved the world…so that everyone giving themselves to the Son may not be lost in their pursuit of happiness in this lifetime alone but rather possess within the gift of Life lived in the now, timelessly."

Focusing deeper, I choose to understand the meaning of John 3.16 like this:

"God so loved the world…so that everyone giving themselves to the Son may not be lost in their own pursuits of happiness in this lifetime alone but may also be given the inner gift of being present in the Now, timelessly."

Keep in mind that the word translated as "eternal life" can often mean "full" or "complete" and "unending." In fact, one of the most important things to realize is that there is an adjective of quantity, and an adjective of quality! It seems to me that the preaching of salvation and eternal life have focused solely on the "quantity of time" in the future, in a paradise called "heaven."
Considering these grammatical insights, I choose to understand this passage speaking about the quality of life – the abundant life that is possible now in relationship with the Triune God through the life, death, resurrection, ascension and sending of the Spirit of Jesus the Christ.

Notice how this deeper translation shifts us away from the language of "getting, receiving, accepting, taking Jesus?" as the language of salvation.

Also, notice how this opens a deeper dimension of understanding: we consent, we surrender, we give our self away to the Source of light, life and love and in this giving (perhaps this is a little death process of the false self), we discover the truth of what Jesus taught: you must first become like a little Child to enter the kingdom of God. You must first die to yourself to live.

A "Salvation" Story

Just in case you are thinking this is purely theoretical for me, please know this is also deeply personal. Here is a bit of my story.

At seventeen years old, I had a "conversion" experience during an "altar call" at a self-defined "Evangelical" Christian resort in the Adirondack Mountains of New York on a Sunday morning in late August 1989.

I do not recall the sermon or the preacher's name, but I recall the experience, especially the emotions and profound awareness of God's cleansing, drenching love.

The near mystical experience certainly changed my life psychologically, intellectually, and yes spiritually.

At the time, I also thought it "saved me" because I "accepted Jesus into my adult heart." Something I had done also as a younger child, perhaps many times.

But this time was different, in part because of the developmental milestone of becoming an adult near eighteen, and the crossroads of seeking for the purpose of my life so common in late adolescence.

Not only did my "conversion experience" give me a whole new spiritual purpose for life it also rewired my consciousness, literally changing me over night.

Just one example. After three years of high school, I had a 2.7 GPA. When I got up from the floor of that sanctuary, flooded with what felt like a waterfall of light, it was as if my mind was switched on, and I returned to my senior year with a hunger for learning, reading, knowledge and wisdom. Where did this new person come from?

Certainly, everything good in my life is a result of that event of total grace encountering the love of the Triune God through the preaching of a faithful pastor inviting me to give my life more completely to the living Jesus Christ.

Today, looking back on over a quarter century of life as a "born again Christian" I can definitively say without question that whatever happened to me when I "gave my life to Jesus" during that altar call was certainly not complete salvation.

There is still much more of Peter that needs to be saved, healed, and transformed. That is the first way I came to see salvation differently. Whatever it is we mean by the word "salvation," for me it is no longer just a one-time event; it is an ongoing, developmental process. As the Eastern Church fathers fondly say, salvation is transformation.

Step #3
It is OK to see salvation differently, Part 2

"Know that, by nature, every creature seeks to become like God." – Meister Eckhart

"All creatures seek after unity; all multiplicity struggles toward it – the universal aim of all life is always this unity." – Johanes Tauler

This chapter follows up from the previous chapter on seeing salvation differently. There, I shared several questions that troubled me about the "salvation style" of Christianity that I was nurtured in during my twenties within self-defined "Evangelical" contexts.

In this chapter, I intend to track three of the more important shifts that helped me grow beyond my prior understandings of salvation without leaving Christianity altogether. Since this is primarily an autobiographical approach, I make no claim to this being a superior way.

It has just been my path, and I wish to share it in the hopes that it might be helpful to others as well as lessen the sense of being alone on a difficult journey. Perhaps, one of the most intimate and important journeys one can make – the spiritual journey, from one degree of understanding to the next into an ever-deepening union with Christ.

First shift: the Fall

My first shift was a re-understanding of the "Fall."

Christian theologians call the source-problem of humankind "the Fall." We look at ourselves, we look at human history, we read passages of scripture like Romans 5, and we can easily conclude: "things are not the way they are supposed to be!" What went wrong? This leads us to look for an explanation as to why things are the way they are.

The traditional explanation (or diagnosis of the problem) offered is that the first human beings disobeyed God's command (Genesis 3.1-7; Romans 5.12).

As a result, they "fell" away from God and lost their intimacy with God, and that somehow in this process of falling away from God the human species and all human social systems became deeply flawed, or fallen, capable of violence, murder and wickedness – all consequences of living separated from God. In sum, as Milton put it, paradise was lost.

What I came to see is that perhaps it was sup-posed to be lost. Indeed, perhaps it needed to be lost for the whole experiment of humankind to ultimately become its destiny.

This new perspective emerged slowly. At first, I was highly influenced and enchanted by the writings and ideas of Ken Wilber.

While you may not agree or like everything Wilber has written, there is no doubt in my mind that his model needs to be taken seriously by, and put in conversation with, Christianity.

(This has been done recently by pastor Paul Smith in his book Integral Christianity: The Spirit's Call to Evolve. And one cannot forget the profound work of Pierre Teilhard de Chardin). Wilber has synthesized several academic disciplines into an integrated evolutionary model of human development accessible to the layperson.

The model is called AQAL – an acronym representing the terms All Quadrants, All Levels. You don't have to agree with Wilber's presuppositions or solutions (i.e. remedies) to see the usefulness of his diagnosis of the human problem.

But in my view the implications of his ideas are so far-reaching they cannot be ignored. And, as far as I can tell, his ideas have been ignored by virtually every mainstream "evangelical" Christian writer and thinker I have read in the last two decades, although recently Brian McLaren's work seems to be aware of Wilber's ideas.

I was particularly helped by Wilber's books, *Up from Eden* and its partner *The Atman Project*, both earlier efforts that are developed further by Wilber's masterpiece, *Sex, Ecology, Spirituality: The Spirit of Evolution*. This is not the place to evaluate Wilber's ideas. I am just sharing that Wilber was one of the most important steps on my journey of seeing salvation differently.

If you are struggling with one level of Christianty, I highly recommend reading Wilber. It will jump-start a terrific internal conversation. In the spirit of full disclosure, please bear in mind Wilber is coming from a very different perspective than traditional monotheism.

I was captivated by his ideas at first, especially the idea that the Fall wasn't a fall downward from a higher perfected state, but was a fall upward, from a pre-personal, pre-conscious state into a fuller, waking consciousness in which humankind could realize the sheer terror of the situation of being human.

Prior to "the Fall," Wilber suggests we did not know or realize our predicament because human consciousness was blissed out in a pre-personal conscious paradise, like an infant fused with its mother's breast. This was a pre-rational, pre-self-conscious Eden, something of which the Genesis story is trying to convey in its limited, pre-scientific way.

Wilber's hypothesis made a lot of sense to me and synthesized multi-academic disciplines such as sociology, anthropology and psychology. Wilber's hypothesis, in sum, is that while it appeared to the first human beings that they had "fallen" to a lower level than the one they first came into being in, actually, the Fall was necessary for their continued growth upward into the image and likeness of God.

It was a developmental transition that felt like a deep separation from God to the first one's who experienced it and therefore it was expressed in such a way in ancient literature as a Falling down. It turns out it was a separation all right, but a separation like waking up from sleep.

We move from the unconscious bliss of union with our Eternal Ground of being, and into the conscious state of awareness that is human existence and freedom – awake, alive and caught in the awkward state of being self-aware, with all its shame, guilt, longings and possibilities.

However, as much as Wilber's ideas have helped me, it wasn't a complete answer. I felt it wasn't representing the goodness and joy of the Christian invitation, nor fully embracing the fact that God probably did create something good. Perhaps even too good, even surprising God by our freedom.

I can just hear the Divine singing in the universe: Oh My, What Have We Done! O My What Shall We Do! And that led me to an ancient idea called theosis.

This evolutionary/developmental view could never have happened for me without first experiencing what I wrote about in the second step on the journey of seeing the Bible differently. Perhaps critics will say, ahh, Peter, that is the root of all your problems.

Be that as it may, I'm so grateful to have come across this developmental perspective of the Fall because it opened me up to vast new insights and spiritual joys, and became the interpretive key that has unlocked the narrative arc of the scriptures into a vibrant clarity held together by the movement of Triune love holding the center of the cosmos until Christ is all in all.

Second shift: Theosis

From Wilber, I naturally moved deeper into one of the most important yet forgotten doctrines of Christianity, well-articulated by Eastern Orthodoxy yet nearly ignored (until recently) in the Western church. I came to see the primary purpose of human existence as theosis, or divinization. And that salvation isn't really in its full flower without it: theosis.

This expanded the salvation narrative beyond just "believing information about what Jesus did for my "salvation" and "entrance into heaven," and opened it up toward a developmentally deeper purpose and fulfillment of why humankind exists in the first place: to grow in ever-deepening union with Christ so to "become a participant of the divine nature" (2 Peter 1.4).

Considering the process of theosis (which has deep resonances with many of Wilber's ideas of human development), the Fall became much more than an event wherein humankind and human nature was "separated from God," it became an allegorical template of the developmental beginning point that we each repeat from birth.

Humankind was created to live at a higher level of being, but the process of birth means that we each begin as little seeds from which each of us is given the opportunity to grow into the full stature of Christ (Ephesians 4.13).

Will we grow and flourish, or will we wither and die? Will our life become full of purpose and meaning in relationship to Ultimate love, or will we spend our lifetime in the far country, rich or poor, totally unaware of who we are and what we could become?

Since Jesus was not only our savior but also the Way, he provided the template by which we too must travel: birth, baptism, discipleship, testing, suffering, death, resurrection and ascension. In one sense, the second person of the Trinity also had a Fall – it's called the Incarnation. Thus, to be the God-man, a separation from the divine was required to enter into the full dimension of planet earth and human nature. This terrifying sense of separation occurred for Jesus, finally, on the cross when he cried out for the first time in his life from the level of human consciousness that is fully separated from God, "My God, My God, why have you forsaken me."

Perhaps you too have been there. Thomas Keating reminds us that in the Garden of Gethsemanene Jesus still calls God Abba, but in this moment of separation on the cross, that intimacy is gone and it is simply raw, human agony: God, where are you? If that doesn't capture the human state of consciousness feeling separated from God I don't know what would. For the second person of the Trinity (the Logos) in the person of Jesus, this required infinite humility (John 1.1-4; Philippians 2).

Whatever the reasons for and causes of the Fall – both ultimately impossible to know with certainty – we can discover that each human life must recapitulate the journey of the Fall from the paradisiacal union of pre-personal awareness, and fusion with the mother in the womb or at the breast and fall upward into the unfolding levels of human potential and growth. Discovering ourselves thrown into life slowly coming to self-consciousness, we are given the gift of becoming. What will we become?

Our journey is growth. Our purpose is becoming. It's about transformation by moving from one level of development to the next, from infancy to adulthood, and then to completely surrender into God at death.

The problem is that many human beings stop developing at the rational-egoic level of human development that we call adulthood, or even late adolescence. We simply become "life" people, and not God-people. Life and all its demands and responsibilities and distractions eats our energy, casting a spell of deep sleep over us as we go about our life pursuing our pleasures in mostly rote ways.

It's because of this that people flock to religion. They are really looking for a way out of the sense of meaningless. They are looking for Divine union with Christ and a journey into transformation, but what we so often give them in the church is a product called salvation, garbled with archaic language about a blood sacrifice, a cross and a savior that bore all our sins. Considering everything I have shared so far, doesn't that message ring somewhat incomplete and not compelling?

This is why Jesus invites us to pray that the divine kingdom would come on earth as it is in heaven. He invites us to pray this because mostly the divine will is not being done on this planet because human beings cling to their sense of separation, power, control and needs rather than awaken to the reality that in Christ nothing can ever separate us now from God (Romans 8.38 – 39), despite all appearances to the contrary.

If we would have the courage to let go of our grasping onto the product of salvation, we might discover again the miracle of what we already are: God-seeds, ready to grow deeper in union with Christ.

Biological life on this planet is not Ultimate Life; it is indeed less than what we are destined for by God. We are created for the unionization of earthy bios and divine breath, flesh and spirit.

Yet, so much of our life is all too often spent sleep-walking through life numbed by all the adult pursuits that culture and even religion promise will help us, but in the end are incomplete programs for happiness leaving us short of the interior ascension and city of God promised to those who are filled with the Spirit as temples of God created for growing "from one degree of glory to the next" (2 Corinthians 3.18) into the body of Christ.

Theosis is God's kiss to humankind, inviting us deeper and higher and broader and wider than we could ever imagine. It is the song of transfiguration calling to us from the cloud of Mount Tabor that there is more for humankind to become.

We are here not just to become Christians, we are here so we can become participants of the divine nature, truly alive human beings. We can become, in the words of C.S. Lewis, "little Christs." We can become love.

Of course, we are not born the Christ as Jesus was. What happened to Jesus by right, happens to us by grace. We are re-born in union with the "Christ-ness" of Jesus and through this process we may reach a level/state of being whereby we can say with St. Paul, "it is no longer I that lives, but Christ in me" (Galatians 2.20), or affirm that we too "are in labor pains until Christ is formed in me" (Galatians 4.19).

For further reading on theosis, I recommend the book Theosis: The True Purpose of Human Life by Archimandrite George.

Third Shift: the spiritual journey

Within the Evangelical culture, the word "salvation" became an umbrella term that covered a multitude of meanings and theological concepts. Here are some of the other words that were used (in my experience) as virtual synonyms of salvation: Redeemed, Righteous, Justified, Saved, and of course, Born Again.

The upshot of these terms is that salvation meant "getting saved," and that this was a "belief event" with ongoing effects that was initiated with some sort of response to the "preaching of the Gospel," and was directly related to "receiving or accepting Jesus Christ as one's personal Lord and Savior."

What we were "getting saved from" was "a life of sin," "a life of separation from God," and especially, "the consequence of hell and eternal judgement." Receiving Jesus, (i.e. believing in Jesus) was the primary solution to all this, as well as the many problems of being a "sinner." But wait, there was more!

After I did receive Jesus as my personal Lord and Savior, I also needed to do other things to get the full benefit of the salvation event. Such as: Read the bible. Pray. Go to church. Worship and fellowship with other believers, and most of all tell other about Jesus. This style of messaging Christianity became problematic for me and created a deepening hunger for Wilber's ideas and the promise of theosis.

Thus in time my understanding of salvation became less about a moment in time; less about information I believe; less about avoiding eternal punishment in hell. Rather, salvation also became about my transformation by God's triune grace, mercy and love into God's image and likeness through an ever-deepening union with the living Jesus Christ and a participation in the union of Jesus' human and divine natures, which was and is Jesus' Christ-ness.

Remember, the definition of Christ is the union of the human and divine in the one person Jesus. Theologians call this the hypostatic union. It's what made Jesus more than just Jesus the carpenter/wisdom teacher.

The Christ-ness of Jesus is the union of Jesus' human nature with the Logos' divine nature in the one person we call Jesus of Nazareth. He's the new Adam, the template of what we are meant to become.

Now, here is where it gets really, really cool: my/our human nature by its union through word, sacrament and prayer with the divine nature hidden in the living Jesus Christ becomes by the power of the Holy Spirit and the will of Abba, a lifelong journey of healing and restoring the divine likeness in me, leading me deeper into the abundant life that is a paradise regained here and now.

From this perspective, salvation even became for me less about Jesus' "finished work on the cross" and all the ghastly dimensions of the predominant atonement theories and questions, and much more about Jesus' entering into and absorbing the fullness of the human condition and the fullness of human nature and not avoiding any of it.

Instead, Jesus went all the way down into the depths of our human condition and experienced the worst of it in its violence, hatred and death not to call it naughty or bad, but to absorb it with love, tears and forgiveness for the sole purpose of healing it through his absorption of it.

This is why Jesus died on the cross – so to bring divine love all the way down to the darkest basement of human nature, and even beyond, into hell itself, so to raise it all up with him and return it all to the heart of the Father's love. This is called the Great Exchange. Jesus assumed everything about human nature to heal it all.

This also means that the goodness of the "good news" is that there is nowhere you can go, nothing you can do, where Christ hasn't' been and therefore there is no one beyond "salvation."

Since the incarnation of Jesus as the Christ, the healing of human nature is now available to humankind by connecting each individual up to the living, resurrected Jesus Christ, but also by following the Way of Jesus Christ – the way of love, self-surrender and giving oneself completely to "the Father's will."

This is the spiritual journey and the best modern articulation of this journey, and all its nuances and psychological dimensions, is the teachings of Father Thomas Keating, especially his book Invitation to Love or the DVD video series The Spiritual Journey.

That there even was a journey beyond my own personal life journal was news to me as a young Evangelical. To my detriment, I had never dared read, for example, St. John of the Cross. Had I, perhaps I would have realized there is much more to the Christian life than just believing in Jesus, reading the bible devotionally and having a good prayer life, etc.

It wasn't until my own life began to fall apart in my early 30's that I realized there must be more to the Christian life than just believing and receiving Jesus and memorizing bible verses. Perhaps I'm over-simplifying and overstating that point.

Nevertheless, in time, I began to realize that one of the unintended flaws with Protestant Christianity's founding presupposition of sola fide is that we are clearly NOT saved by faith alone if salvation is measured by any standard of human social behavior or psychological growth. At least I wasn't. Granted, if salvation is simply defined as the ability to get into heaven, then perhaps we are indeed just saved by faith. But that is something we can't know here and now. And I know far too many supposed heavenly bound Christians who haven't moved very far beyond self-righteousness on the journey into becoming love.

I don't mean that as a judgement, but rather a simple statement of fact. It's the only way I can comprehend the fact that it took until 1964 for (at that time) the primarily "Christian" nation of the United States of America to pass the Civil Rights Act, and even then, according to well-known historical accounts some white Christians and churches still despised "black people."

This is a colorful example, yes, but it makes my point well. We've got a world full of people who say they are saved after 2000 years of preaching the Gospel, but the world doesn't seem to be getting much better. Hmmmmm. I wonder why that might be. Do we spend energy blaming everyone else, attacking the "liberals" or whatever else we might think is "an enemy of righteousness," or perhaps we might begin to look at our own understanding of our salvation message and discover that without the aspect of participation in the divine nature, perhaps our preaching of salvation is inomplete?

Missing, perhaps, the psychological dimension so well-articulated by Wilber and Keating. For my life, and from my perspective we have an urgent need to rediscover salvation's full flowering: theosis.

What we can know and measure, is how people are transformed after a "salvation event." In my personal experience, since 17 years old, my "salvation event" left plenty of room for an ongoing sanctification journey.

By God's grace, it's a journey I'm still saying Yes too, despite my doubts and fears. In the silence, I'm often reminded, "my perfect love casts out all fear." For me, a daily practice of meditative prayer – Centering Prayer or the Jesus Prayer have been integral to the unfolding spiritual journey, and the primary way I taste and see the oneness of union and the next step to becoming love. I will write more on this kind of prayer in step #5.

Again, I'm on my journey, so I don't have the last word. Verify everything in the light of your own interior space for grace where Christ's impressions are felt in Word and Silence.

I'm simply sharing where I have come from, not particularly where I am or where I will be. May it birth further love, light and life, and not foster negativity, darkness or despair. God is with us on our journeys into the heart of divine love through the process of theosis as we are being raised in Christ to the radiating Taborian light of Triune love.

For further reading on this view of Christ that I discussed above, I recommend starting with Raimon Pannikar's book, Christophay: The Fullness of Man or my book, The God Who Is Here, especially chapter three. For further reading on the ontological view of salvation wherein Jesus assumes everything to heal it, you might start with the writings of T.F. Torrance, especially The Mediation of Christ.

Step #4 It's OK to See the Earth Differently

"Space has a spiritual equivalent and can heal what is divided and burdensome in us." – Gretel Ehrlich, The Solace of Open Spaces

"The views of nature held by any people determine all their institutions." – Ralph Waldo Emmerson

We continue with step #4 – It's OK to see the earth differently. This follows very nicely from step#3 seeing salvation differently, since so much of the "Evangelical" message of salvation I heard was often solely heaven focused, tacitly denigrating the earth as "just the place where we live until we get to heaven," or the place that will be replaced with the "new heavens and the new earth."

From Forestry to Ministry

I have felt deeply connected with the earth. It is almost a romantic connection, marked by longing, desire and awe. I need to be in the wilderness. I feel calmed by pine forests and inspired by mountain ranges. I love the smell of the earth on Spring and Autumn days and often retreat to the forested shores of Lake Michigan or Lake Superior for solace and renewal. My spiritual life is deeply nourished by wilderness, and the beauty of the earth. I don't overromanticize it though; it's a fierce wilderness with a power over me.

The vastness of the forests and mountains could consume me whole, by raging weather, or hungry or frightened predators such as wolf, grizzly or mosquito.

After high school graduation, my plan was to become a forest ranger. I was accepted at a great college for such an endeavor. Northland College in Ashland, Wisconsin on the shores of Lake Superior provided me with the perfect setting to pursue this interest. But something happened to me the summer prior to my freshman year.

I sensed a call to the ministry. After my first semester of college at Northland, I decided to switch tracks and leave Forestry and enroll at Moody Bible Institute in Chicago to become a pastor. Over a few months, I went from the vast beauty of the Apostle Islands and the Porcupine Mountains, to the densely energetic downtown of Chicago.

Just to survive in that urban environment, I made it my practice to walk the five blocks from Moody to Oak Street Beach, where I could get a view of Lake Michigan, and escape the crowded noise of the city. The contrast between the two worlds was sharp. I don't think I could have endured Chicago or Moody without Lake Michigan, and the little hidden parks that preserved a sense of peace for me.

During my four years at Moody, I started to become much more bookish. My sense of wonder was smothered, and a pervading sense of fear and dread invaded my thinking and feeling.

This sense of fear and dread was directly related to the atmosphere of religious intolerance toward anything that did not embrace the theological vision of that environment.

It became for me a very cold and controlling place, intellectually dissonant with my warm heart. In my head, I heard the demand for salvation through Jesus alone and the need to preach this Gospel to everyone lest they go to hell. In my head, I heard the rules and regulations for curfew, dress code, and non-tolerated behavior such as movies or masturbation.

But in my heart, I knew that in the vast beauty of the wilderness, such dictates did not seem to be so present, and that the beauty of nature seemed to convey its own message of salvation and freedom in its own profoundly silent way to all who might listen.

The best way for me to describe the outcome of my experiences at Moody was that while I did indeed learn a lot and was deeply formed in many positive ways, I recognized that I was out of whack, and I couldn't put my finger on why until I got back into the mountains and woods and realized that my experiences with Evangelical culture in the 1990's had somehow led me to disconnect from the earth and my body.

I was malnourished living in the city of doctrines, withering on the vine due to my long absence from the garden of wonderment and simplicity. Not only that, but my physical body also took a severe toll. I was physically malnourished having eaten a steady diet of primarily processed cafeteria food for the better part of four years.

Early on following my "conversion" at 17 and 4 years at Moody, I began to experience significant physical problems such as digestive disorders, acid reflux, and severe back pain. It wasn't until I started Yoga practice 10 years later that these (what I now view as psychosomatic disorders related to the culture of fear and control) went away.

This suggested to me that not only did my Evangelical spirituality tacitly disconnect me from the earth, it also disconnected me from my body. This is a subject we will explore further in Step #6, but I found the Evangelical rejection and fear of the earth and body very curious and similar.

The route back to wholeness and balance began after I left the city and was able to have more daily access to parks and nature.

Such places restored my soul and body and brought me back to balance, sometimes daily. Places like Lapham Peak Park in Delafield, Wisconsin and the vast old growth nature preserve behind the Institute for Advanced Study in Princeton were refuges for me during the years after I left Moody and downtown Chicago.

My experiences with the earth and its seemingly healing affect upon me gave me reason to believe that there was more to life than just knowing and believing in the right doctrines. And this led me to explore the life-giving writings of Annie Dillard, Wendel Berry, Eugene Peterson, Sallie McFague and more recently Ilia Delio and Belden Lane. Also, the importance of the book of nature within the Reformed tradition was one of the primary attractions I had to the Presbyterian Church USA, and it was a rescue line to me helping me leave the distorted dualism of the Evangelical culture I experienced during my college years.

What is so curious to me is that while on the one hand the Evangelical spirituality I was exposed to had such a literal, high view of creation – that God created everything is 6 days – in practice, there seemed to me to be a widespread distancing from the earth, and a resistance to the ecological movements grounded in stewardship and sustainability. I can recall hearing a professor talking about the "evil agenda" of earth day.

I can remember listening to student conversations about our consumption of earth's resources as being our divine right, regardless of what effects it may be having on our planet. And I can recall the outright rejection of any science that tried to show that human behavior was having an impact on global climate change.

Today, 35 years from those college conversations, the Evangelical community has come a long way on its views of the stewardship of the earth. Perhaps not far enough though. Here are some ideas on how we might go journey deeper and farther together toward a more life-giving, balanced and spirituality integrated ecology so often embodied by Benedictine monastic community.

Relationality In Community with All Bios

In my book, *The God Who Is Here*, I have a chapter on re-envisioning how we build our churches and do church community from a contemplative perspective. Here is a brief selection:

Contemplative Christian community places itself in humble reverence and relationality to and with all life—human, organic, animal, cosmic, Divine. Contemplative Christians have intuited that love leads to union and reverence.

The ecological movement isn't just a modern phenomenon; once, religious traditions lived in deeper harmony with the natural world. While some choose to only see this as paganism, I wish to remind them that God is the God of all life and the creator of all creation. Why would anyone choose to live separate from the creator or the creation? Such thinking comes from one who divides by fear, not one who binds together in love.

Contemplatives understand that reverence is not worship. We don't worship mother earth or Gaia, but we do consent in deep reverence to the reality of our interrelatedness.

Once again, science can describe the "what" and "how" of this interconnectivity, but our purpose here is to highlight the "why." The contemplative answer to this question is that we live in reverence to all life because all things come from God.

Recall that in the beginning God spoke and said let there be light (Genesis 1). The ancient story of Genesis is intended to convey to us the nested hierarchy and interrelatedness of life. What is it that binds all of this life back to God? Yes, love — but beyond love is the Spirit of God infusing the entire cosmos and creation with Christ!

The contemplative dimension of Christianity wishes to order its external life bound to this reverence for life. In this way, we live with humility, lest we think we are the source of our life.

While life requires effort against what appear to be the chaotic forces of nature, wisdom leads us further into a harmonious way of being with the creation. It's the contemplative disposition of reverence toward the creation that's of vital importance to re-claim in our Christian communities.

In this third millennium of Christian faith, we're blessed to contemplate the repository of insights gained by those who have preceded us. One such legacy burns more luminously than others — that of Francis of Assisi. St. Francis lived during a time of cultural transition; the "dark ages" were slowly ending and the Renaissance would emerge within a hundred years of his death.

His "Canticle of the Sun," sometimes also called the "canticle of creation," conveys a simple understanding of the interrelatedness of all things. This song-prayer beautifully summarizes our whole point of reverence for life:

O Most High, all-powerful, good Lord God, to you belong praise, glory, honor and all blessing.

Be praised, my Lord, for all your creation and especially for our Brother Sun, who brings us the day and the light; he is strong and shines magnificently. O Lord, we think of you when we look at him.

Be praised, my Lord, for Sister Moon, and for the stars which you have set shining and lovely in the heavens.

Be praised, my Lord, for our Brothers Wind and Air and every kind of weather by which you, Lord, uphold life in all your creatures.

Be praised, my Lord, for Sister Water, who is very useful to us, humble and precious and pure.

Be praised, my Lord, for Brother Fire, through whom you give us light in the darkness: he is bright and lively and strong.

Be praised, my Lord, for Sister Earth, our Mother, who nourishes us and sustains us, bringing forth fruits and vegetables of many kinds and flowers of many colors.

Be praised, my Lord, for those who forgive for love of you; and for those who bear sickness and weakness in peace and patience — you will grant them a crown.

Be praised, my Lord, for our Sister Death, whom we must all face. I praise and bless you, Lord, and I give thanks to you, and I will serve you in all humility.

The Canticle of the Sun conveys a non-dual, intergral awareness of the interconnectivity of all things, as well as the reverent place humanity inhabits: we crown creation not as monarchs, but as surrendered servants who live in reverence for and adoration of the One from whom all things come and are presently moving within, and who will one day return.

Reaching this point, we're now ready to go beyond envisioning characteristics of what a contemplative community could be, and into the realm of spiritual evolution, which is in essence a process summarized by our prayerful intention for an increasing correspondence between heaven and earth.

The means by which this spiritual evolution occurs is a form of grace, drawing us further into God's intentions. It's a graceful movement propelled by the attraction of Divine love to the creation. It's love that draws us into the Divine destiny and fulfills the mystery of who we shall be. It's Divine love that will make us complete. Scripture summarizes this vision with great beauty:

May the God of peace . . . make you complete in everything good so that you may do his will, working among us that which is pleasing in his sight, through Jesus Christ, to whom be the glory forever and ever. Amen. (Hebrews 13.21)

It's wise for Christian leaders to consider how this internal contemplative dimension might take shape in external, structural ways. For example, how can the church manifest God's relational presence with more integrity and congruency in our buildings? Could our buildings demonstrate our commitment to relationships and community better? Could they manifest a creative and symbiotic relationship with creation that leads the way for ecological and social sustainability and stewardship?

I believe the answers to these questions can and must be yes! We now explore a few ideas on just how we might envision contemplative community in this very practical way.

The Beauty of Relational Buildings

If we are to manifest the presence of God through our community life, we might consider designing campuses that more intentionally manifest the relational presence of God. Such a vision for our churches is rooted in the relational theology of the Trinity, and an implementation of the relational and theological principles of the incarnation.

Instead of undertaking building projects that create a "one-stop" destination for spiritual services (worship, education, ministry), why not envision structures that foster community living and ecological stewardship? For example, envision a church redeveloping several downtown blocks. With that space the church could fashion not just a building, but a functioning community where day by day, home by home, business by business, the relational presence of God could be manifested to the surrounding communities as people lived in tangible community.

This is one way in which our function as the relational presence of God in community could take physical expression as a living spiritual ecosystem incarnating the presence of God through life, light, and love, which ultimately is beautiful itself.

The church would become a community where members could live, work, play, and worship. It would be a way of being community with intentional designs impacting physical structures and architecture.

It's not a new vision, rather a re-visioning of the parish community that emerged with the development of churches in the center of village life. It's also a vision shared by the monastic communities who desired to demonstrate in tangible forms something of the function, form, and flow of the kingdom of heaven here on earth.

If this vision is criticized as social engineering or communism, I would argue that it's no different from what many city planners are designing for trendy sites in urban centers and gated communities. City planners have already begun building towns with community and relationships in mind. The oil and ecological crises have added urgency to such developments. But most of all, it's our culture's tacit longing for community and meaningful relationships that is driving such market shifts.

There are critiques to this kind of community design. The first is that we further inculcate a defensive isolation from others not like us. To counter this, I imagine interracial communities that commit themselves to reconciliation and relationship. The second danger is that these communities become Christian subcultures.

My response: Each community could also host people of other faiths. What we gain in terms of quality of relationships and communal life far outweighs the perceived risks of spiritual mingling. Such risks forget the understanding of Christ's eternal presence and action before, beyond, and after the historical incarnation as Jesus.

The entire missional church discussion is also in agreement with the church's need to move outward, rather than inward. Such a re-imagination of the form of church buildings supports this outward vision in that the church community actively seeks to live among the world as a people demonstrating the relational presence of God in all our form and flow. I don't see the "village" or "parish" church model in contradiction to the missional church model. Rather, combined, they balance and strengthen each other.

The missional church emphasizes that the church doesn't exist in buildings but is an outward movement of people in relationship with Christ, participating in Christ's work of love and grace. However, at the core of all our Christian faith is the claim that "the word became flesh" (John 1.14), thus the incarnation gives clear permission to enflesh the light, life, and love of Christ we experience with imagination, intentionality, and beauty in how we design 0Christian community.

While community is counter-cultural to the American sense of independence, and while many examples exist of the dangerous extremes that can occur in spiritual community (such as the Branch Davidians), the Christian church, at its heart, is a communal experience grounded in relationship—with God and with each other.

Relationships take form; community takes shape. Why not form and shape a village that visibly demonstrates and enacts relationships and community, and that is dedicated to spiritual transformation through worship and spiritual practices?

The church building can be more than a mall or a one-stop destination for spiritual services. The church can be a living, enfleshed community, designed and structured with aesthetic beauty, ecological sustainability, and relational reverence, like a spiritual ecosystem.

The Beauty and Flow of the Weekly Sabbath

The seven-day week is central to Christian spirituality. Grounded as we are in the Jewish tradition, it was the Christian shift from a Saturday to a Sunday Sabbath that bears a compelling witness to the resurrection of Jesus. The shift is also more than historical.

The Jewish notion of a day of rest is rooted in the creation story where we're presented with God's activity of creation segmented into specific days: but on the seventh day, God rested.

The narrative structure of the book of Genesis provides a basis for ordering time in a week, and it's the week that's the essential framework within which we are to establish a rhythm of relationship as well as a Christian spirituality. All the activities and spiritual practices that nourish our relationship with God such as prayer, reading of scripture, private and public worship are placed within the weekly, seven-day framework.

Sunday is the hinge day between weeks. It's the day of recollection and visioning, the day symbolizing the in-between age we live in now. We go about our rhythm of relationship throughout the entire week, not just one day. Creativity emerges over the whole week, lived daily.

In the Benedictine monastic tradition, each day is a miniature week, broken into seven time periods, some for work, some for prayer, some for rest and fellowship. Each week, like each day, has a beginning and an end, marked by the cycles of light and darkness—as the Sabbath evening approaches, the week is drawing to a close, and as the Sabbath day concludes a new week is emerging.

Therefore, the reality of relationship emerges through the daily disciplines of the entire week, deeply connected to the rhythms of the earth and its relationship to the sun, moon, and stars; light and darkness; season and cycle.

Yet, it's Sunday that consummates the Christian week. Not just because it's the symbolic day of renewal and rest, but because it's the last and first day of each week. It's the day of transition and symbolically bears witness to the resurrection. Similarly, Sunday is very much like the hours between dawn and dusk: the day of remembrance and anticipation. Sunday hinges the week that has passed with the week to come.

During this time of reflection and envisioning, we have an opportunity to renew in worship and detect the spiritual relationship with the cycle of the earth and allow our own beings to be nourished in rest, community, and time in nature.

Beauty and Seeing All of Life as Worship

The incarnation affirms the value of being human and doing human things. Our spirituality shouldn't diminish our humanity or lessen the glory of the physical body. Our spirituality attends to our bodies, aware of the interconnection of Spirit to our own energy, breath and physical well-being.

The rhythm of relationship is one way in which we're transformed as individuals and as a community more into the image of Christ. Through our bodies, the earth, and our communities, God is working, ministering, and indeed, present. The liberating and joyful message of the incarnation is that we can glorify and manifest God in all we do. All of life can be sacred.

The liberating message that God is relational as embodied in Jesus is that the life of Christ returns our humanity to God and brings the kingdom of God to us, here and now.

It's interesting to note that even with all our progress in communications technology, we long for community, connectedness, close and caring relationships with others more than ever.

However, because of the nature of our communications and commuter-oriented society, we live with the awkward tension of being more connected than ever and simultaneously being starved of authentic, enduring, and meaningful relationships. So, what is it that we are in need of? What would such a community look like? What is community in the first place?

With such questions in mind, consider M. Scott Peck's suggestion that true community is "a group of individuals who have learned how to communicate honestly with each other; whose relationships go deeper than their masks of composure, and a group of people who have developed some significant ability to rejoice together, mourn together, delight in each other, and make other's conditions their own."

This is the essence of Christian community — dwelling together in love and vulnerability for the sake of manifesting the presence of God to one another and the world.

This vision challenges our culture of separation and transience. If we are to nurture and demonstrate meaningful relationships in community, and if we are to demonstrate the presence of God, we as individuals and as the church are invited do at least two things:

Provide a sense of real presence amid diversity, separation, and isolation. Real presence is essentially attentive, close, and caring relationships committed to intentional covenants and sincere reconciliation enacted in ritual and manifested in love. Another way of saying this is that we live sacramentally, bound by the internal bond of self-giving through faithfulness and forgiveness.

Provide a sense of permanence amid transience and non-commitment. Permanence is the willingness to remain and endure even at personal sacrifice. The vision is for meaningful communities grounded in the commitment to be a rooted presence in a specific place with specific people, providing emotional, financial, physical, or educational support as it may arise.

An excellent book to read on this subject of developing an ecological spirituality is Care for Creation: A Franciscan Spirituality of the Earth by Ilia Delio, Keith Douglass Warner and Pamela Wood. Also, Jonathan Wilson-Hartgrove is doing a wonderful job articulating monastic principles for community living. Check out his excellent book The Wisdom of Stability.

Step #5 "It's OK to See the Prayer Differently"

In this chapter I will share several highlights from my journey into a contemplative prayer practice, and how I began to see prayer differently from the "evangelical" environment I grew up in.

When I was a Freshman at Moody Bible Institute I began an intense prayer practice. In the common area of my dorm, there were four prayer closets. I would go there at 4am to pray. At first, I followed the ACTS pattern of prayer: Adoration, Confession, Thanksgiving, and Supplication.

I earnestly prayed for hours at a time, and often fasted. During the first months of my second semester, I began a prayer group for revival based on 2 Chronicles 7.14.

By my sophomore year, I began to develop my own pattern of prayer. I still have and sometimes use the notebook that I wrote the pattern in. Here are a few of the categories:

Unto God

Confession of sin

Silence

Adoration

Exaltation

Thanksgiving

Renewed Submission and Followership

Invocation of the Holy Spirit

Fruit of the Holy Spirit

To increasingly know You and Your truth

To increasingly love others
Relationships
Family
Physical needs
Governmental leaders

During my junior and senior years at Moody I worked at the Crowell Hall reception desk. I worked the 4:00am – 8:00am shift. I specifically requested this shift so that I could have time to pray in the morning.

Since there was nothing to do from 4:00am – 6:30am I used that time to pray and study. At first, I sat in the quiet darkness of the early morning and went through my prayer list. I always felt renewed after my prayer time but began to notice that feeling quickly disappeared as the day progressed. I noticed that despite my hours of prayer and scripture study, the peace and sense of connection with God in my "quiet time" didn't always seem to translate into a peaceful Peter going about his day.

I also noticed another thing. Some mornings as I slowly and quietly went through my prayer list, I discovered that I would drift off into silence, or what I thought at the time was sleep. I felt guilty when this happened because I wasn't finishing the prayer list and I would "come to" and discover an hour had passed.

However, I also sensed that I wasn't asleep. I knew I was awake, but I was deeply resting and deeply at peace, and I felt warmth in the center of my chest area.

While I wasn't praying with my mind using my list, somehow, I sensed I was still praying in my spirit. What I had stumbled upon and did not realize was the gift of contemplative prayer. It would take several more years to discover that there was a method and model of such contemplative prayer, and that it had been a part of the Christian spiritual tradition since the beginning.

I had stumbled upon the ancient Christian practice of the prayer of the heart taught by the desert fathers and deeply embedded in the pre-scholastic monastic tradition. But because I had at that time no historical or theological understanding of what that contemplative tradition might be, I continued to deepen my intensity of my petitionary prayer life.

As a result, I have 15 journals full of written prayers, some quite long. All expressions of devotion and requests, for my own life or for others.

After graduation from Moody, and during my subsequent seminary years, my intensity toward this kind of petitionary prayer life ever so slowly began to wane. I noticed that my level of energy was just not there. I felt guilty about this and heard voices of conviction shaming me that I had "backslidden" and that my devotion had grown "lukewarm." Looking back now, I know that was not the case.

What was happening to me was the normal occurrence on the spiritual journey of developing from a spirituality primarily grounded in my sense of self, to a spiritual life primarily grounded in the diminishment of the self and the emergence of Christ. This sometimes feels like one is losing one's faith because one is no longer connecting to God in the ways one used to.

When one's sense of self is the primary connection to Christ, it feels terrifying when this self begins to go away and one is left, in a sense, naked in faith, alone with Christ. I wasn't losing my faith; I was losing parts of my false self. I was growing deeper into faith. And a part of this growth was releasing myself and my sense of control that I felt through my prayer practice.

Many people experience a similar cooling of intensity of faith and prayer. It is normal. One of the reasons is because we are designed to move from the petitionary level of prayer to the contemplative, resting level of prayer. We are designed to move from praying to being prayed. From asking to surrendering.

From requesting to consenting. From making claims in the name of Christ, to resting in the presence of divine love. From just following Jesus, to becoming a participant in the divine nature.

One of the problems I experienced on my journey was that much of Protestant Christianity, at the time, did not have a framework for helping me move forward.

My options at the time were, return to my petitionary intensity or not, or move into the liturgical expression, where petitionary prayers are replaced by more written expressions of prayer. And that is what I did. I let the liturgical tradition carry me when I couldn't carry myself. And I found great refuge, comfort and inspiration in the liturgical renewal of Christianity. This too was one of the reasons I chose to join the Presbyterian Church USA. And yet while liturgical, devotional, written prayers often touched my emotions, they also seemed to stay up in my head – meanwhile something in me was longing for deeper union and experience.

In the late 1990's I was also helped by the writings of Richard Foster and Henri Nouwen, both of whom pointed to a deeper way of being Christian, but both of whom did not specifically teach or write about a contemplative prayer method.

During my first three years as a pastor, I continued my morning prayer practice. But instead of my petitionary prayer list, I simply read a scripture and then sat in silence with a light blanket over my head.

I did not usually fall asleep, but I did simply rest in the silence of my heart, meditating upon the words of the scripture, and letting my heart rise in adoration or petition as it did. I did not try to think about what I was praying. In this way, I began to cultivate the experience of being still and knowing that God is God (Psalms 42.6). I also began to read the beautiful writings of Thomas Merton, who began to open me more broadly to the contemplative dimension of Christianity, although he too was lacking a specific method of contemplative prayer.

Centering Prayer

My prayer life was forever transformed in 2003 when I came across a simple little book (of method!) written by Thomas Keating called Open Mind, Open Heart.

Through Keating's writings, I discovered that there was a name and long-standing tradition to what I had stumbled upon in my own practice as a younger man in college. It was called contemplation, and it could be nurtured through the method of prayer Keating and others called Centering Prayer.

There are other similar models, such as the Jesus Prayer, which is simply saying a variation of this: Lord Jesus Christ, Son of God have mercy upon me a sinner." Or even simply, Jesus, Mercy. But the method/model I came to practice and that has been a means of God's healing grace for me is Centering Prayer.

The method of Centering Prayer is very simple and is designed to foster our consenting to God's presence and action, the simple resting in faith. Here is a brief overview of the four guidelines of the method of Centering Prayer from Contemplative Outreach, Keating's teaching organization:

Choose a sacred word as the symbol of your intention to consent to God's presence and action within.

Sitting comfortably and with eyes closed, settle briefly and silently introduce the sacred word as the symbol of your consent to God's presence and action within.

When engaged with your thoughts, return ever so gently to the sacred word.

At the end of the prayer period, remain in silence with eyes closed for a couple of minutes.

Centering Prayer is a method of silent prayer that prepares us to receive the gift of contemplative prayer, prayer in which we experience God's presence within us, closer than breathing, closer than thinking, closer than consciousness itself.

This method of prayer is both a relationship with God and a discipline to foster that relationship. Centering Prayer is not meant to replace other kinds of prayer. Rather, it adds depth of meaning to all prayer and facilitates the movement from more active modes of prayer — verbal, mental or affective prayer — into a receptive prayer of resting in God.

Centering Prayer emphasizes prayer as a personal relationship with God and as a movement beyond conversation with Christ to communion with Him. The source of Centering Prayer, as in all methods leading to contemplative prayer, is the Indwelling Trinity: Father, Son, and Holy Spirit. The focus of Centering Prayer is the deepening of our relationship with the living Christ. The effects of Centering Prayer are ecclesial, as the prayer tends to build communities of faith and bond the members together in mutual friendship and love.

Today, I practice this prayer twice a day for at least 20 minutes. I take a 10-day centering prayer retreat each year. It's like getting a spiritual oil change.

Through this prayer practice, I have experienced, beyond my control, deep levels of personal healing – emotionally and spiritually. It is a living miracle what happens when we simply sit down, shut up and consent to the divine presence and action in the silence. In fact, I can say that this prayer practice has held me together as a human being, and as a pastor.

Without it, I would have left the pastorate. Centering Prayer, or any meditative, receptive, resting prayer is how divine grace puts a fine point to our personal transformation and healing into the fullness of our God intended destiny as co-heirs with Christ.

Yeah, but…

Yeah, but isn't this new age? Or Buddhist? Isn't this too Catholic, and not Protestant? I'm sure you can find many objections and critiques of Centering Prayer. But let me ask you something, how is your prayer life?

If your prayer life is transforming you, deepening your sense of peace, wisdom and love, if you are receiving deep rest from your prayer practice, by all means do continue. But if you hunger for something deeper, if you are looking for peace in this culture of information and busyness, perhaps you might be interested in the contemplative way.

In my view, it is an ethical imperative for the future of humankind on planet earth overflowing with 7 billion people and counting for Christians to return to the heart of Jesus' teaching: when you pray, go into your inner room and close the door and pray with your Abba in secret (Matthew 6.6).

How are things on planet earth? Perhaps now more than ever we might wake up and realize that something different could help us. Something the sages of every religion have been trying to demonstrate and teach – that our freedom and future may just depend upon our return to the silence where the Spirit of God can hover over our chaos and birth the new creation.

For those readers who may wonder about how "Protestant" this prayer is, let me say this. From a Reformed Protestant perspective, the contemplative, mystical path seemingly took a backseat to the emphasis on justification through faith, especially through the faithfulness of Jesus Christ and his work on the cross.

However, Calvin does deal with this subject matter, although he uses different presuppositions and terminology than Keating. For Calvin, any transformation we experience is grounded in the secret working of the Spirit who mediates God's presence and healing in us, always through our union with Christ. By faith and baptism, we're plunged into the loving and living waters of God.

This is what it means to be "baptized by the Spirit," a life-giving and transforming infusion of Divine life, light, and love in us. We know that this transforming infusion occurs because we begin to increasingly long for a deeper, fuller, more immediate experience with God.

The longing is compelling evidence that the gift of God's presence and action is "spilling over" into our hearts and minds, and quickening us to love, serve, worship, and seek after God in prayer and action.

For Protestants, union with God is made possible through union with Christ. So, what does "union with Christ" mean? It means that we know who God by what is God does, and God has been doing quite a bit of revelation.

To the best of our knowledge, God has chosen to be a relationship as Father–Son–Spirit, and to send forth to humanity the Son, who is Jesus Christ, to be for us and our salvation the very manifestation of God among us. This Son, Jesus, would himself show us (reveal) who God is and teach us the way to know and experience God.

Jesus taught us to change our way of life and to believe in him; that to know him was to know the Father. By surrendering to Christ, one could receive the gift of his Spirit and thereby be united to God through Christ the Son by the power of the Spirit. Could there be any better way to surrender and consent to the presence and action of the Trinity than resting in sheer faith in the silence.

Could there be any better way than embodying sola fide than to incorporate into your prayer life a little silence and surrender of self? There is a widespread resurgence of Reformed thinkers returning to the doctrine of theosis.

The books to read are: *Union with Christ: John Calvin and the Mysticism of St. Bernard* by Dennis Tamburello and *Theosis: Deification in Christian Theology* by Vladimr Kharlamov and Stephen Finlan.

The Future

I deeply believe that it's only a matter of time before the renewal of Contemplative Christianity is main stream.

A widespread personal and corporate incorporation of a meditative prayer life is, in my biased view, the primary hope for the main line church and will be the primary refuge when people burn out on the high-octane, self-focused mega church carnival ride.

If, as the first century theologian Irenaeus said, silence is God's first language, perhaps after all these centuries of human tumult, violence and war, as well as all the centuries of progress, technology and human growth, it is urgently time for us to return to the contemplative path of prayer to help us both prevent our self-destruction and embrace our full potential. May God help us awaken to the gift of silence hiding in plain sight, awaiting our attention and return to the home of our heart.

Step #6 It's OK to See Sex Differently

As with the previous chapters of this book, my aim is not so much to be right, but rather to become love. If something I write does not serve love, please forgive me. Since becoming love is a lifetime journey, there is always more to learn; this is certainly not the last word on human sexuality. Perhaps these reflections are therefore only an incomplete pastoral reflection, yet I pray, perhaps still useful.

A Story

I begin with a true story that illustrates some of the tensions I experienced around sexuality within an Evangelical Christian environment. In 1992, during my sophomore year at Moody Bible Institute, the Dean of Students was inspired to host a men's and women's assembly – separately – to discuss sexuality. I can only imagine what the women's gathering discussed. I know what the men heard though.

All the men gathered on the bleachers in the gym of the Solheim Center. I'll never forget what happened next. For about 30 minutes the Dean of Students discussed why masturbation was not permissible biblically and that Moody men were not allowed to masturbate. Our bodies, he said, had a natural way of dealing with our buildup of sperm, called wet dreams.

I am not kidding. I was in shock, and I don't think I was the only one shocked, since the gym was dead silent, and afterward my friends just kind of looked at each other as if we were all thinking, "did that really just happen?"

Looking back, I realize this isn't a Moody thing. I don't resent Moody or the Dean of Students at all. I see them as innocents caught in a much larger system of confusion and repression infused within much of Christianity for centuries.

This story is an example of the anti-sexual and even anti-body bias in the guise of "spirituality" and "holiness."

That is nothing new in Christianity. What saddens me about so much of Christian culture, especially the Evangelical culture I experienced, is that there was little to no capacity or willingness to integrate spirituality with sexuality apart from the extreme measure of abstinence and chastity until marriage.

For me, this created an unhealthy, unbalanced pressure cooker and the inevitable feelings of shame and guilt when the normal surge of sexual energy was activated or enjoyed.

An example of this pressure cooker at Moody was that women and men weren't allowed in each other's dorm rooms. So, occasionally, walking in the basement hallways or in a darkened classroom one might be surprised to walk in on a horny young couple making out or having "dry sex." There was just no place to really fool around at Moody.

The place was pretty much locked down – including dress codes and curfews. I'm certain that's why some parents loved sending their kids there!

It wasn't just at Moody either. In my experience in every self-defined Evangelical church and context I participated in, sexuality and spirituality were completely disconnected. A practical dualism reigned, inherited most likely from Pauline texts of scripture pitting "flesh against spirit," and perhaps even a hangover from the writings of St. Augustine, who was overly harsh on the body and sex given his own feelings of shame and guilt about his past sexual life that he abandoned when he became a Christian.

It's all so unfortunate. People whose whole religious foundation is built upon the Word becoming flesh (John 1.4) should be the first to embrace our bodies and sexuality integrating and including sexuality into our spiritual journeys, versus sequestering it away with fear and shame.

I have much to share on this subject of sexuality and Christianity from a personal perspective, but it would not be wise for me to do so in writing or in this public way.

That is sad to me because I think until people start sharing more vulnerably and truthfully from a personal perspective Christian culture will continue to remain at an immature level of sexual integra-tion. I believe that it's often when we tell our stories that shame and fear latent in the system can begin to be exposed and healed. Until we do, the dominant nar-rative will be set by our culture, and our youth are listening carefully.

Unfortunately, what they so often hear from the church isn't a beautiful vision of integration of sexu-ality grounded in love, but legalistic generalities grounded in fear.

Sadly, it seems to me that too many of our Chris-tian communities are still not safe places to be vulnerable and honest about human sexuality – whether you experience yourself as straight, lesbian, gay, bisexual or transgender.

It's as if we all pretend, we don't have a sexual life except when someone else has a "problem" with theirs. Then we often act as if they are the only ones with a sexuality.

The truth is we are woefully ill prepared to have a meaningful conversation about sexuality today, es-pecially if our only resource is the Bible. Without in-sights and data from the psychological, developmen-tal and medical sciences, any discussion on human sexuality today is virtually irrelevant and potentially damaging.

What I will share here are five principles that have come to me over 20 years of reflection, reading, prayer and conversation on the subject of human sexuality.

Loveless Sex

In my view the intent of the scriptures that speak to human sexuality (and there are not many comparatively speaking) is loveless sex – the kind of love-less, anonymous, throwaway sex that occurred in the Greco-Roman world at bath houses, brothels and temples with wiling partners, prostitutes one paid, or temple servants one simply used. Such loveless sex was called *porne* sex, where we get our word pornography from. *Porne* is the opposite of Agape love. Agape love is self-giving, other focused, and loyal.

The principle of loveless sex was that you can't just use someone as you please. Spiritual sexuality is grounded in love for the other not taking from the other to meet your own needs exclusively. Love nurtures mutuality and self-giving, versus taking and self-absorption.

Eros love was erotic love, and it differs from *porne*. Eros love is passionate sexual love. *Porne* is not love at all. It is loveless, lustful consumption selfishly seeking to satiate one's own desire. The problem with that is that only Agape love can truly satisfy erotic desire.

Only when Agape love is united with eros love do we truly experience the fullness of human sexual satisfaction. The two are designed to run together, but they so often run separately due to the power of lust co-opting and overriding our physical energy channels and brain neurons.

The interesting thing about defining the problem of sexuality as loveless sex is that I have a hunch there are lots of monogamous marriages where loveless sex happens all the time. In the sweep of Christian history, how many "good Christian men" have used their wives lovelessly?

By the high divorce rate and the marriage counselling sessions I have listened to, I think it is a large number. Perhaps we should ask the women about this the next time there is a big church conference on human sexuality? This is where Jesus' question is instructive: "Who among us is without sin…" (John 8.7).

It's instructive in any conversation about sexuality and Christian leadership because I think there are many instances where church leaders overlook the loveless sex occurring in their own lives only to focus on what they fear or don't understand happening in someone else's sexual life.

I received a word from the Lord on this subject: Everyone is a sexual being. If you are human, you are sexual. This is about all of us. And eros sexuality is more than your genitals or act/s of sex. Everyone is also a spiritual being. If you are human, you are spiritual.

All of us. And spirituality is more than the act/s of belief or worship. Christians don't have a copyright on the spiritual nature of being human. Human beings, by nature of being a human, are de facto also spiritual beings.

This is God's doing. Similarly, Agape love is not copyrighted by heterosexuals. And eros love is not copyrighted by homosexuals. In practice though, in many Christian circles, there is an unwillingness to see the possibility and presence of agape love in non-hetero relationships. The rationale, so they say, are a few passages from scripture.

I suggest a more in-depth study of those passages, because none of the so-called prohibitive passages are dealing with a quality of relationship grounded in agape love.

They are dealing with *porne* behavior – loveless sexual acts, not committed loving relationships. It is worth pondering the distinction.

We would also do well to begin to move beyond defining relationships by the kind of sex they have to the quality of the love they share. Human beings are more than our sex.

And our sex, sexual orientation and preferences seem to vary across a wide spectrum – from very hetero to very homo, and everything in-between, including the genderless and the bi-sexual. This is a fact of human biological evolution and won't be going away and can't be ignored by burying our heads in the sands of ancient scripture.

It seems wise for mainstream Christianity to find a narrative rooted in love in order to interact with the reality of the multiplicity of human sexuality. A narrative that is more workable than just saying, "don't do this or that."

To help us focus on nurturing such a more workable narrative, Christianity could develop a love-based sexual ethic versus a gender-based sexual ethic. While the ancient scripture announces that God created them "male and female," (Genesis 1.27; Mark 10.6) what we now know is that there is a spectrum in-between the masculine and feminine poles, and each of us over the course of a lifetime may shift on that spectrum, even if subtly.

This is a function of hormones changing in our bodies and it is one of the reasons (just as an example of this complex process) why Viagra is so popular – it helps aging men retain more of their sense of maleness, while nature, left without Viagra, is shifting many toward a more neutral state.

Lust

I wish we would also shift our conversation away from sexual orientation and toward the presence of lust in our sexuality. In a "50 Shades of Grey" culture, we might find the spiritual wisdom of dealing with the power of lust useful.

Lust is the wanton desire of someone or something. Lust is a powerful energy/thought that can inspire behavior. Evagrius Ponticus, a 4th Century monk, ascetic and teacher, developed a useful teaching for the monks who spent a great deal of time in prayer and solitude.

The monks began to realize that even though they were in solitude, the mind was populated with temptations and thoughts, what Evagrius called *logisimo*. These thoughts were described as provocations, and came to be developed in eight categories, what we now call the "seven deadly sins."

When tempted by a "deadly thought" or energy such as lust, perhaps an image would come to mind. Or perhaps a physical sensation would rise energetically in the body. Thoughts, they discovered, preceded behavior.

The remedy was not to go along with thought. Not to believe the thought. In this way, one could move through the provocation and not engage them. This added practical meaning to the Pauline invitation to connect the sanctification of our bodies with the "renewal of our minds" (Romans 12.1-2).

Each of us, no matter our sexual orientation is a spiritual being. And each of us can be tempted to lust. The temptation is often specific to each of us.

Our temptations are tailor-made by our minds, our repressions, our early formative impressions and experiences, or in some instances, an external spiritual energy interacting with your mind and body. I would like to see heterosexual Christians and homosexual Christians talk more about the power and presence of lust in their sexuality.

I think it might be a very useful way to level the playing field so to speak. I think it might be helpful for many Christians to hear gay Christians admit there is an issue with lust in the gay lifestyle, and it might be very helpful for gay Christians to hear heterosexuals admit the presence of lust in their marriages and sexuality, as well as a tangible lack of love in the church.

Perhaps such confessions would be good for fostering open conversation and honest dialog. Perhaps I ask too much.

Lust tends to deplete us energetically, whereas love tends to fill us.

One of the reasons lust keeps people coming back for more is that, while it may be titillating and thrilling, it is often not ultimately satisfying; whereas eros love infused with agape love has a way of deeply satisfying.

I tend to think people go to the bar and have a one-night stand not because they are bad or drunk, but because they are longing for love. Perhaps it's the longing for love and deep intimacy that drives them to the bar and bedroom in the first place.

But, despite its powerful allure, lust has a way of depleting us and not giving to us what we deeply desire, which is love.

Lust also has a way of accepting the superficial as normal and simply using another's body for one's own pleasure. Having said that, loving sexuality, eros, can and should be passionate too.

Love based sex doesn't need to be boring or dull. I view lust and passion differently primarily because in my pastoral experience it is lust that has seemingly brought the most damage and pain to people's lives, and erotic passion that often brings lasting love and joy.

It is a very subtle difference that can't really be described, only experienced. The book to read is *Passionate Love: Keeping Love and Intimacy Alive in Committed Relationships* by David Schnarch.

Love precedes being – including all ways of being.

We move from lust to philosophy by starting with an important philosophical question and presupposition.

What comes first – Being or Love?

Some say that Being comes first, and from this the human experience of love evolves. In that case, Being precedes Love.

But others say Love comes first. In that case, Love precedes Being – which is what the doctrine of Divine Creation implies. God is Love and creates all Beingness or all possibility of Beingness implicit in the "Big Bang."

If Love precedes and is the Source of all Being, then it follows, to my mind, that Love precedes all ways of Being too, which is also the philosophical rational for not judging others.

This reality of love preceding all ways of being is further strengthened in the light of the Cross event of Jesus Christ. In the cross event we can make a strong case that any judgment the Divine may have had toward humankind, or our continued infantile, nonloving behavior was absorbed by the innocent self-giving love of the Son. What was he doing on the cross? Jesus was embodying the pouring out of love as the innocent victim demonstrating the absolute absurdity of the human way of dealing with judgment and fear by violence – emotional or physical.

And God allowed it to play out not so much to be "satisfied by a blood offering," but so that the divine nature could unite itself all the way down to the very depths of our human nature – the depth of our violence and rejection of love.

Jesus absorbs our absurdity of religious judgment, non-love and violence with tears and forgiveness, ultimately giving himself in surrender to the mystery of the One he called Abba.

From this point forward in human history, as symbolized by the rending of the temple veil, divine love precedes all ways of being liberating us from the need to try to play God with the various ways of being human, including being human sexually.

The deep shame of the church is that we have continued to use violence – verbal, emotional, physical – as a result of our playing God role, thinking we know best or that we need to purify, or eliminate, or mandate, or separate from those we think deserve God's judgment or whose way of being somehow disqualifies them from the infinite circle of God's love.

At one point the church did this to the Jews, sometimes the Muslims, sometimes women, certainly slaves, and today it is still occurring in far too many Christian communities toward, those who identify as LGBTQ.

I don't mean to confuse gender with race. Or sexuality with slavery. They are totally different. When it comes to sexuality, we are dealing with something deeply embedded in our beingness and as such how much more so does it need to be met with love.

If, in the process of living and loving people discover that they need help or feel "broken" sexually, they will seek healing in communities that practice love grounded in the principle that love precedes all ways of being.

The gift of forgiveness is possible for anyone, and in forgiveness, so too is healing, which each one discovers in their own way and time. Healing, especially any healing in our sexuality, is one of life's deepest mysteries and can't be manipulated or controlled.

Healing unfolds. And sooner or later, almost everyone starts seeking it. We can trust God with these deep mysteries. The Christian community that gets the message of love in Christ and practices it through forgiveness will be a compelling community to welcome the coming tsunami of sexual woundedness that is arising all around us in our porn-saturated-web mediated-lust crazed culture.

This will require of each of us hope, faith and love – learning how to tolerate one another and bear with one another's different manifestations of being on our unfolding journeys into deeper healing. Letting the peace of Christ rule in our hearts and the rule of love guide us, are the primary means of covering a multitude of ways of being that are not our preference or that we might label less than ideal. This is not easy to do.

Remember, the great way of love is easy for those without preferences. And a contemplative prayer practice can help foster the no preference way of being. It can usher us into a state of union where love unites all.

Here is one upshot of this philosophy. Perhaps it would be wise for us to cease playing God with human sexuality and let God be God. This may apply to both sides in the church – those resisting the future and those fighting for change.

From there, we can focus on loving one another and the spiritual practices that nurture such love, such as contemplative prayer and lectio divina.

Energy

It's important that you hear me when I say one of the primary fruits of daily meditation or a contemplative prayer practice is that it begins to heal our deeper divisions of self, including our deepest desires and shames hidden in our sexuality.

The contemplative tradition is full of sexual-love mysticism images. This isn't just poetry. The mystics are trying to convey the interior experience of sanctification and deepening union with Christ, which often travels on the same wiring our sexuality uses, and can also heal and release our sexuality too.

This may be surprising to some, especially sensitive young souls seeking to be devout to God, who discover a powerful world of sexual forces within them.

One of the most interesting fruits of a meditative prayer practice is that the grace of the Spirit of God can release that which is repressed in us and help us integrate that energy for an ever-deepening and maturing spiritual life in Christ.

If our sexual energy remains repressed, wound-ed or misused, we may miss the fullness of spiritual life, which is abundant, life-giving and empowered as an integrate whole being.

One of the problems of a dualistic approach so typical in Christianity is that it kept the body separate from the Spirit. Doing so often dams up one's erotic energy, creating a potential disaster should that sexual energy break loose suddenly or in an inappropriate context, surprising all involved. One of the most important remedies to such a problem is the slow integration of sexual energy into the divine energy of the Spirit through a meditative prayer practice.

In my experience of contemplative prayer, one of the deepest and most powerful human energies can get released in us in the silence of surrender, and that energy is eros – that is to say, it is the primal energy coiled up at the base of our spine.

The Vedic tradition calls this the Muladhara Chakra. Unfortunately, in Christianity we don't have a good understanding of the energy centers in our bodies. In this case, it is important to learn from our brothers and sisters and their wisdom traditions of the body.

Yoga is helping many Christians reconnect with their bodies and discover a language to describe their personal experiences with this energy. A good book to read about this energy and the role of a contemplative prayer practice is Kundalini Energy and Christian Spirituality: A Pathway to Growth and Healing by Philip St. Romain.

In Christianity, the primary energy flowing through the body is viewed to be the Holy Spirit. But the Holy Spirit does not ascend from the base of our spine.

The Holy Spirit descends upon people, anointing them from above. This divine energy can then flow into the human body starting with the crown chakra at the top of the head and moving successively all the way down to the base chakra at the tip of our spine. But if there is a blockage or repression of some sort in us, this divine energy may sometimes get blocked, and we may experience this blockage in the form of pain, twitching, or other sorts of physical symptoms.

Good body work, such as deep tissue massage, yoga or chiropractic work can help in this process of integration. In the Vedic tradition, the lower energy can be activated so that it rises. This is different from the energy of the Holy Spirit. It is eros energy.

Since every human being has eros energy coiled at the base of our spine, integration can occur when the divine energy of the Holy Spirit unites with our human sexual/eros energy. This union is perhaps what happened to Jesus at his Baptism (Luke 3) after which he was immediately led into the wilder-ness temptations, and from there a ministry of mir-acles.

I believe it was because of the complete spiritual integration with his physical energy – the union of Holy Spirit energy and Eros energy (i.e. Kundalini) – that he was able to endure and overcome his temptations. Of course, interiorization of the scriptures was of great help to him in this process too.

Perhaps Jesus was fully embodied and knew the experience of energy flowing into him from above and up through him from below (Luke 8.46).

There is a good case to be made that the activation of his healing powers was because the Holy Spirit descended upon him and integrated with his rising eros energy. As such, he was in total balance, a picture of what humankind is supposed to be too.

Unfortunately, the kind of Christianity many of us experience and that I experienced growing up was essentially disembodied. Unbalanced. All Bible, no body.

Although, on a side note, the charismatic or Pente-
costal churches seem to get "spiritual energy," but
often too theatrically and disconnected from the wider church tradition of spiritual formation. But their
intuition is correct. They remind the church that we
can and must return to the spiritual energy activated
in and through our bodies by the anointing and fill-
ing of the Holy Spirit.

One of the clearest places we can see the integration
of human sexuality and spirituality is in our energetic experiences of eros, which is primarily an "electri-
cal" type energy that gives us a "charge" toward
something, usually another human body, and sometimes even our own body.

Some spiritual practices, such as "slaying in the spirit" or "healings" are probably indications that the
person doing the "trick" has a much more activated
energy flow, whether it be from the Holy Spirit or
just raw charismatic energy sourced from the root
chakra and its eros power.

It is hard to tell, but we can know a tree by its fruit.
Look for the fruits of love, joy and peace, versus the
fruits of power, control, fear and greed.

Healing sanctification

I have written about my personal story of healing –
physically and spiritually in my book *The God Who Is
Here*, so I won't repeat it now.

What I can say is that it was through a highly "activated" energetic healer that I came into fuller balance and healing. And the follow up from my "healing event" was a weekly practice of Yoga, that helped keep my body-energy moving and in balance.

The healer I encountered bore beautiful fruits of love and freedom in me that continue to this day – 8 years later.

Theologically, this process is called sanctification. Sanctification is not just spiritual. That is a fallacy. Sanctification is spiritual and physical. Our sexuality begins to be healed and transformed into love as our more negative, repressed energies get released to help us integrate our Being into the divine energies of Di-vine love in Christ by the Spirit.

The releasing process can sometimes feel scary or even involve acting out sexually. It is a part of the sanctification process of becoming a "participant in the divine nature" (2 Peter 1.4).

While chastity and abstinence are viable options, they should not be used as a means of escaping the divine wish to integrate your humanity with Christ.

Don't just avoid your sexuality for some spiritual reason. Integrate. Our sexuality just may be one of the most profound means toward a fuller and deeper spiritual healing and wholeness and the resurrection of the body into abundant life in union with Christ.

In this process, there is nothing more important than remaining grounded in prayer, scripture and worship, some fasting, and especially the wise counsel of a spiritual mother or father that you can tell everything to in an environment of love and trust.

Step #7 "It's OK to See Your Destiny Differently

"Blessed are the pure in heart, for they shall see God…" (Matthew 5.8).

Thanks for attending with me through this journey. I pray it has been or will be useful in some small way to your unfolding deeper into Divine love.

The chapter is brief, since it is about the future, and there is little I know about the future except that unless human beings continue to be transformed by divine grace and personal efforts, the future will be much like the past.

The passage of time alone does not imply progress. Without grace, it implies perhaps recurrence, or as the wisdom teacher puts it, "there is nothing new under the sun" (Ecclesiastes 1.9).

For most of my early life as a Christian in self-defined Evangelical contexts the future was, in many ways our raison d'être. I was instructed that people needed to hear the Gospel to know that God loves them and give them the possibility of believing the information that we had (and they did not), that Jesus Christ died for their sins. By believing this information and "receiving Jesus into their hearts" their future would instantly be changed from the certainty of hell and eternal separation from God to the certainty of heaven and paradise in God's presence.

This is what I was instructed – it was the environment in which I lived and breathed, and it created a deep impression of both anxiety and responsibility. I came to despise it, and such presuppositions were a factor in my journey seeking a different way of being Christian.

The problem is that the future is such a big part of the energy of the Christian message. It often seems most "religion" is about both the protection from the risks of the future and assurances of the glories of the future. It's impossible to get away from the future within the Christian narrative or even within the Gospels.

As a pastor, I deal with this issue in real-time. Just yesterday I visited the bedside of a dying parishioner who called me to visit because, in his words, "I don't feel worthy. Will God accept me?" I deal with this at the time of funerals all the time, when it falls to me to put words on the wordless mystery of what happens next, especially to those who every-one knows couldn't have cared less about God or faith during their lifetime.

So, here it is, here is what I both believe and intuit in the silence of contemplative prayer. It is how I see both my past, present and future:

We come from God.

We return to God.

And in between we can learn how to love God and one another.

Of course, some will say there is more to it than that. Yes, more words. More explanation. More theology. More scripture. But, as someone once said, "Explanation tends to spoil the lion's leap." Clearly, the Christ event makes this three-fold maxim possible.

Without the Jesus story, it's less clear how we both return to God and learn to love. Thus, I'm grateful for the evolutionary move the presence of Jesus represents in the "archeological record" or human spirituality. Without the Jesus narrative, we are left in the dark ages, that is without the "light of the world."

The purpose and possibility of each human life is development, evolution, growth into love. Christ is the first-born of a large family (Romans 8.29) and shows us the way to become love in our lifetime.

That's why the Jesus narrative shifts to the Holy Spirit narrative and the possibility of each human being becoming a "temple" (1 Corinthians 6.19) and a "participant of the divine nature" (2 Peter 1.4). Why people resist such a compelling opportunity is a deeper mystery of the human drama beyond my understanding.

Does this make me a universalist? Yes, in this way: we are all in this universe and we can never *not* be in this universe. We are all universalists, until perhaps we die and transition to what might be a different universe. The point is, I can't rule out anything because of the nature of divine love which is beyond us all – a love that seems to patiently tend the garden of earth using biological life to an end we can't completely understand.

Since we don't have complete understanding or know what the ultimate end point of divine love is, we use poetic imagery to convey something of its mystery, terms such as the fires of hell, paradise or the kingdom of heaven.

No doubt, faith is a crucial leap – into this moment, and out of time when we die. But not the only thing. In addition to faith, there is also hope and most importantly love (1 Corinthians 13.13).

Eternal life isn't infinite time; it is no time. It is beyond time. Remember, the word "eternal" can also mean "full" or "complete." One life ends, and a new life begins – a much fuller life than we could ever imagine beyond the spiral of time, which is one of the dimensions of this created universe and not necessarily an aspect of the Divine Being and Love and it's "environment."

I suppose, when it comes to seeing our destiny differently, we shall all see soon enough.

I wish you every blessing on your journey deeper into love and conclude in our family name, the most holy threefold name – Father, Son and Holy Spirit.

Amen.

www.ingramcontent.com/pod-product-compliance
Lightning Source LLC
Chambersburg PA
CBHW070635030426
42337CB00020B/4015